lonely planet KIDS

A KID'S GUIDE TO
LONDON

LET THE ADVENTURE BEGIN!

by Paige Towler

Project Editor: Priyanka Lamichhane
Designers: Carolyn Sewell, Andrew Mansfield
Publishing Director: Piers Pickard
Publisher: Rebecca Hunt
Art Director: Emily Dubin
Print Production: Nigel Longuet

The Lonely Planet Kids Travel Guides series is produced in partnership with the WonderLab Group, LLC.

Special thanks to our city consultant, Tasmin Waby, and editor, Rose Davidson.

Published in May 2025 by Lonely Planet Global Limited
CRN: 554153
ISBN: 9781837585298
www.lonelyplanet.com/kids
© Lonely Planet 2025
10 9 8 7 6 5 4 3 2 1
Printed in Malaysia

All rights reserved. No part of this publication may be reproduced, stored in a retrieval system or transmitted in any form by any means, electronic, mechanical, photocopying, recording or otherwise except brief extracts for the purpose of review, without the written permission of the publisher. Lonely Planet and the Lonely Planet logo are trademarks of Lonely Planet and are registered in the US Patent and Trademark Office and in other countries.

Although the author and Lonely Planet have taken all reasonable care in preparing this book, we make no warranty about the accuracy or completeness of its content and, to the maximum extent permitted, disclaim all liability from its use.

STAY IN TOUCH
lonelyplanet.com/contact

Lonely Planet Office:
IRELAND
Digital Depot, Roe Lane (off Thomas St),
Digital Hub, Dublin 8, D08 TCV4, Ireland

Paper in this book is certified against the Forest Stewardship Council™ standards. FSC™ promotes environmentally responsible, socially beneficial and economically viable management of the world's forests.

lonely planet KIDS

A KID'S GUIDE TO
LONDON

LET THE ADVENTURE BEGIN!

by Paige Towler

CONTENTS

- How to Use This Book — 10
- Welcome to London! — 12
- Mapping It Out — 14
- Getting Around Town — 18
- Places to Play — 32
- What a View! — 46
- Let's Eat! — 58
- Along the Thames — 70
- The Royal Treatment — 84
- The Wild Side — 96
- Going Green — 108
- Secrets of the City — 118
- What's the Difference? — 130
- Index — 134
- Resources — 138
- Credits — 139

IMAGE: The Changing of the Guard ceremony at Buckingham Palace.

How to Use This Book

Are you in search of a city's most delish desserts or wild about urban wilderness? Maybe you want to check out some awesome transport options or discover the history and mysteries of the city. Or, perhaps, all of the above? Each chapter of this book has a unique theme. You can read the book from beginning to end or dip in and out any way you like! Don't forget to scour each page for fun facts, places, people and more.

Like collecting facts and stats?

Check these out.

The busiest Tube station in London is Waterloo, with about 100 million passengers per year!

What makes this city tick?

Explore along the Thames on pages 70–83 or learn more about London's royal history on pages 84–95.

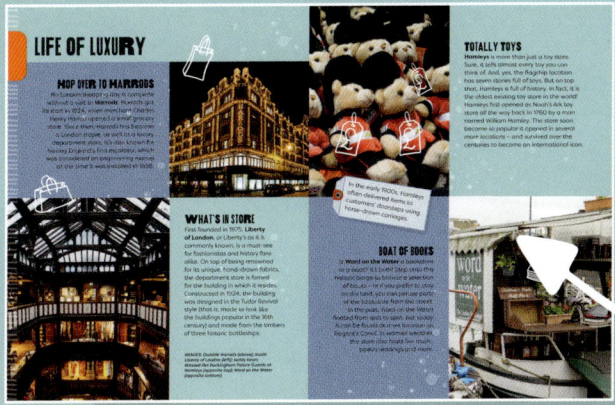

Curious about the weirdest, wackiest and most unheard-of spots?

'Secrets of the City' is on pages 118–129.

Need something to do while waiting for the train, bus, plane, or car?

Look for 'What's the Difference?' on pages 130–133.

Welcome to London!

Whoosh! Double-decker buses whiz down the streets. Underground, the Tube speeds through tunnels. Above it all, palaces sparkle in the Sun. You've arrived in London!

Search for iconic sights like Big Ben, Tower Bridge and St Paul's Cathedral as you take in the scene from above on the enormous London Eye or from the water while cruising the Thames (pronounced TEMS), London's famous river. Visit Westminster Abbey and stand in the very spot where royal coronations are held.

Don't forget to enjoy a visit to Buckingham Palace or stop to people-watch at Trafalgar Square! In London, this is just the start of your adventure. Let's go!

IMAGE: A double-decker bus zooms over Westminster Bridge.

BITE-SIZE HISTORY

There's so much to do in London – and that's partly because there is so much history. Though the site has been inhabited for 4,000 years, the city was officially founded about 2,000 years ago as the ancient Roman city of Londinium.

Mapping It Out

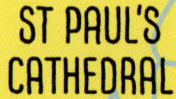

ST PAUL'S CATHEDRAL

WESTMINSTER ABBEY

BIG BEN

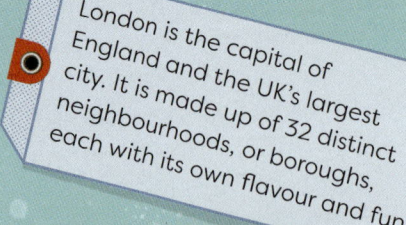
BUCKINGHAM PALACE

HOUSES OF PARLIAMENT

LONDON EYE

RIVER THAMES

London is the capital of England and the UK's largest city. It is made up of 32 distinct neighbourhoods, or boroughs, each with its own flavour and fun.

THE GHERKIN

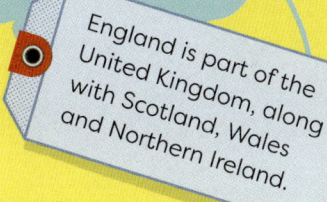
England is part of the United Kingdom, along with Scotland, Wales and Northern Ireland.

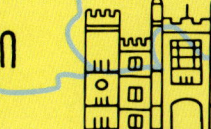
TOWER OF LONDON

TOWER BRIDGE

O2 ARENA

THE SHARD

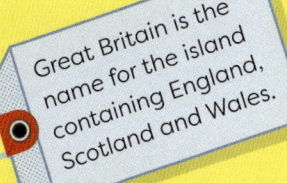
Great Britain is the name for the island containing England, Scotland and Wales.

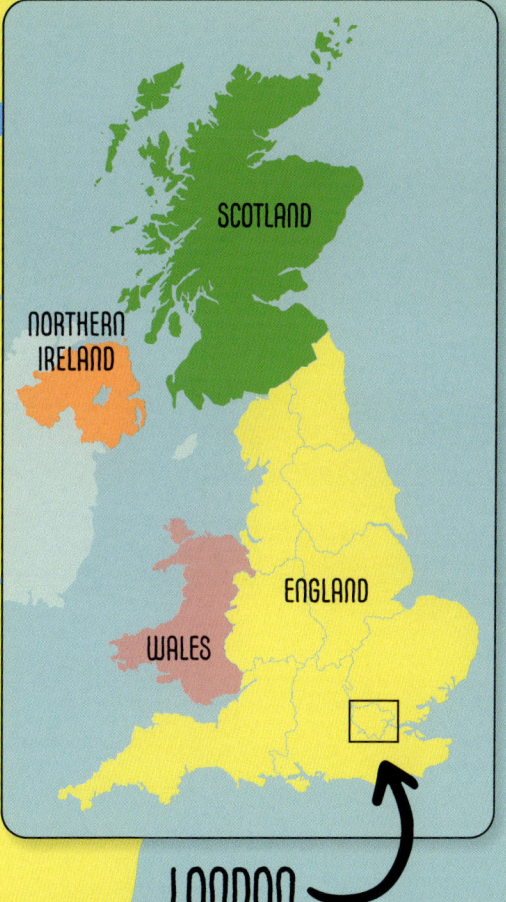
LONDON

Mapping It Out 15

TAKE THE TUBE

With 11 lines and more than 270 stations, the London Underground (the Tube) is one of the most bustling transportation systems in the city. The Tube first opened in 1865. Today, it reaches far and wide, with its longest journey going more than 87 km (54 miles).

Fast Facts

Year first line opened: **1863**

Number of passengers in the first year: **9.5 million**

Number of passengers in 2024: **about 1.1 billion**

IMAGES: Inside Piccadilly Circus station (above); a passenger reads a map of the Underground (right).

GETTING AROUND TOWN

IMAGE: The view from Trafalgar Square.

ON THE GROUND

London has about 675 bus routes and more than 19,000 stops!

DOUBLE IT

Like most major cities, London has a bus network that covers the whole city. What makes it extra cool, though, is that most of these buses are double-decker buses. That means instead of one level of seats, they have two! Today, the city buses are fully enclosed – meaning you won't get soaked when it's raining. But in the early 1900s, they had open roofs.

IMAGES: A double-decker bus (above); an open-top tour bus (opposite top); a taxi on Regent Street (opposite bottom).

HOP TO IT!

On many London bus tours visitors can hop on, hop off. This means that as you take the tour bus around the city, it stops at several landmarks and famous locations. There, you can hop off the bus to check out the sights and stay as long as you like. Then, when you're ready, you can catch another bus and keep going.

The first 'bus' with two decks was actually a horse-drawn carriage.

CALL A CARRIAGE

London taxis have been around for 300 years! They are also known as hackney carriages. It's thought that they got this name from the French word *hacquenée*, used to describe horses that once carried Londoners around the city before cars were invented. Although taxis are called black cabs, not all black cabs are black these days. All you have to do to call a taxi is stick out your arm and hail one!

ALL ABOARD!

UNDER LONDON

To zip from one end of London to the other, the Elizabeth line is the way to go. It took 10,000 engineers, construction workers and others to build this train line. And the effort took 13 years. Why? Because workers kept digging up historical artefacts! These finds included a 700-year-old cemetery, a 300-year-old chamber pot (a portable toilet), ancient Roman coins and much more. The line is named for Queen Elizabeth II.

TAKING THE TRAM

Like much of London's early transportation, trams started out as horse-drawn vehicles. The first tram tracks (for horses!) were built in 1861. Electric trams came about in the city in 1901. Today, there are 45 km (28 miles) of tram lines with close to 30 million passengers every year!

Sometimes also known as a trolley, a tram is a type of train that runs aboveground on tracks powered by electricity, often through the cables that run above it.

There are 45 stations in the DLR system.

TRAIN TIME

The Docklands Light Railway, or DLR, is unique in a very interesting way – it has no driver! The automatic train connects to the London Underground (see pages 26–27) at some of the larger stations to take travellers heading towards the Docklands area and Canary Wharf, two busy parts of town. This train system also played a big role in the London 2012 Summer Olympics: the trains took visitors to the Olympic Park. Due to all the people visiting London at the time, the DLR reached a passenger milestone, with 100 million journeys from 2012 to 2013!

IMAGES: Inside a car on the Elizabeth line (opposite top); the Tramlink (opposite bottom); a Docklands Light Railway train in Canary Wharf (left); a London Overground train (below).

SEE THE SUBURBS

The London Overground, as the name implies, travels aboveground as it visits London's boroughs and suburbs. However, the train line started as a pedestrian tunnel. In 1843, the Thames Tunnel opened – after 18 years of construction! It was one of the first tunnels built under a river. By 1865, the tunnel was bought by a railway company and connected to the broader rail network. In 2024, the lines on the Overground were given new names, such as Lioness, named after the English women's soccer team and Suffragette, after the movement that fought for women's right to vote.

PERSON POWER

HOOFING IT

One of the greatest ways to get around London is walking! Some of London's streets are made from cobblestones, so comfy shoes are a must. The city is made up of an exciting mix of busy avenues and winding, narrow alleys – many of which are famous. What better way to explore places like Abbey Road – the famed site of a photo featuring renowned British band, the Beatles – or the grandly decorated Regent Street than on foot? While you walk, take in historic stone building fronts, hidden cafés perfect for a snack and bright street art.

In central London, you can also ride around in pedicabs: three-wheeled cycles with wide, covered seats.

Fast Facts

Number of Santander Cycles bike docking stations: **around 800**

Number of Santander Cycles bicycles: **more than 12,000**

Year London's first cycle lane opened: **1934**

Lots of walking tours operate around the city, and some even go underneath it! On a London Underground tour, you can explore abandoned platforms, secret tunnels, hidden shelters and more.

BIKES OR BUST

Thanks to its relative flatness, London is fairly easy to get around on a bicycle. Plus, with the city's many canals, parks and riverfronts, there is always new scenery to enjoy. Bicycles are super popular and Cycleways are cycling routes that make it easier for cyclists to get around the city safely. You can even rent bicycles around town! The Green Belt Cycle Route is perfect for kids to enjoy a ride and see some of London's greatest sights, such as Hyde Park and Buckingham Palace.

IMAGES: Regent Street (above); Santander Cycles bicycles for rent (left).

Getting Around Town 25

TRAVEL THE TUBE

Stations on the London Underground, more commonly known as the Tube, are easy to find around town. Look for the famous Underground sign: a red circle with a white centre.

Each year, the Tube trains travel as many miles as it would take to get to the Moon and back more than 2,000 times! The system covers 402 km (250 miles) around the city!

Some of the stations are very deep underground. Hampstead, for example, is the deepest at 58 m (190 ft) below the surface.

The Tube is also full of ghost stations – stations that are no longer in use. There are 40 of them! The Aldwych ghost station is now a museum and is sometimes used for TV or film productions. There are secret entrances and tunnels, too.

IMAGE: A Regent Street entrance to the London Underground.

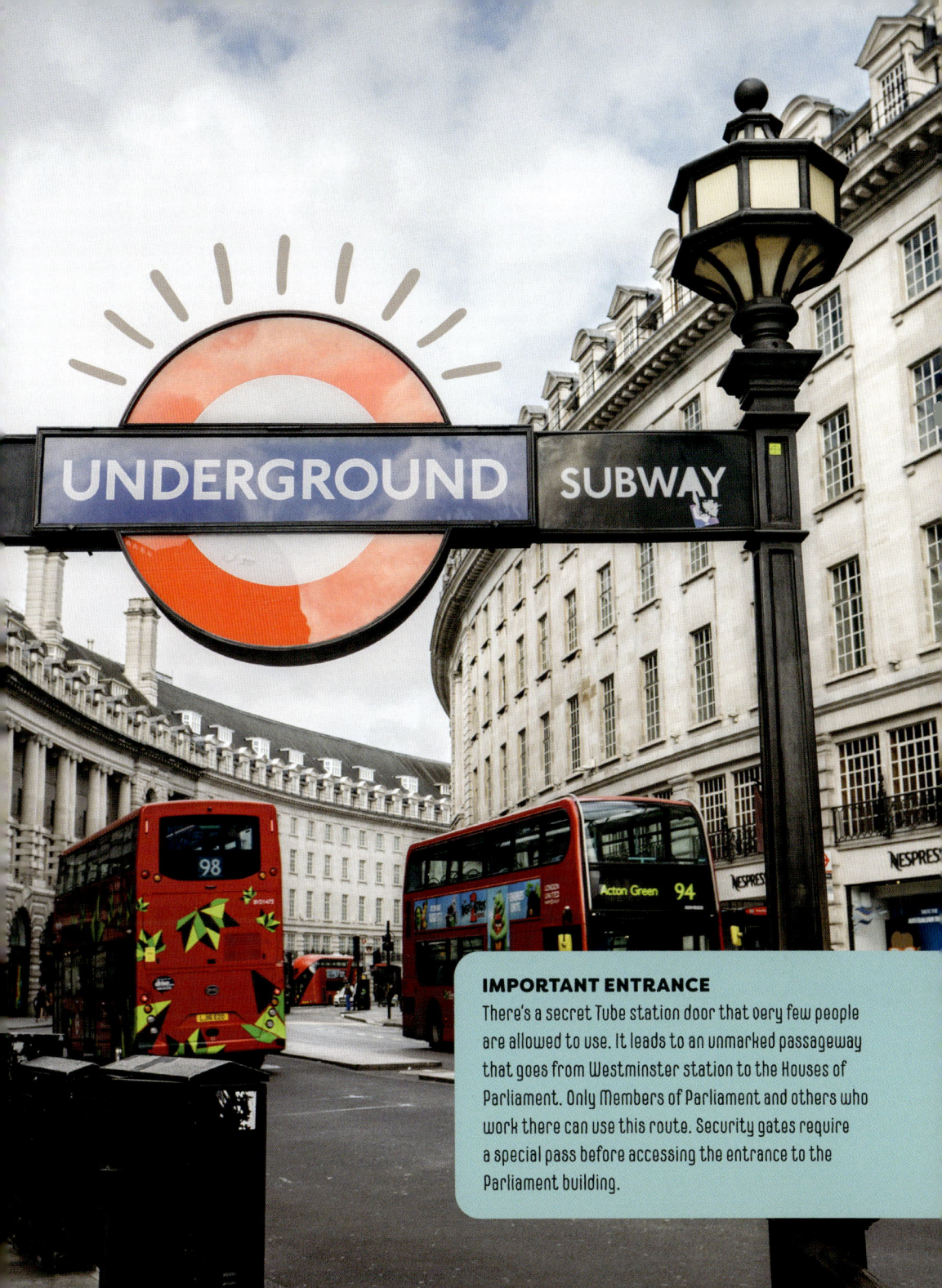

IMPORTANT ENTRANCE
There's a secret Tube station door that very few people are allowed to use. It leads to an unmarked passageway that goes from Westminster station to the Houses of Parliament. Only Members of Parliament and others who work there can use this route. Security gates require a special pass before accessing the entrance to the Parliament building.

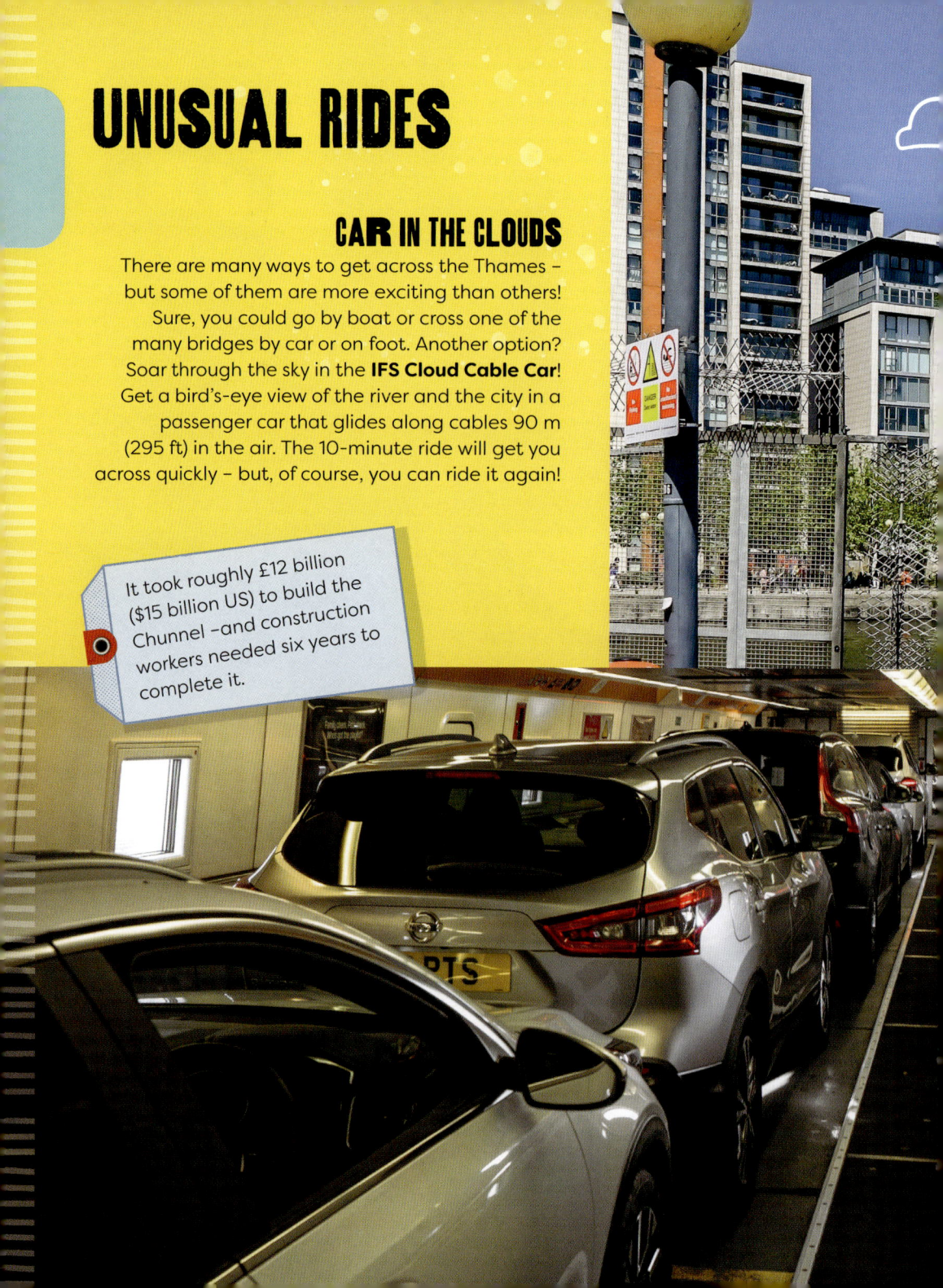

UNUSUAL RIDES

CAR IN THE CLOUDS

There are many ways to get across the Thames – but some of them are more exciting than others! Sure, you could go by boat or cross one of the many bridges by car or on foot. Another option? Soar through the sky in the **IFS Cloud Cable Car**! Get a bird's-eye view of the river and the city in a passenger car that glides along cables 90 m (295 ft) in the air. The 10-minute ride will get you across quickly – but, of course, you can ride it again!

It took roughly £12 billion ($15 billion US) to build the Chunnel –and construction workers needed six years to complete it.

More than one million people ride the IFS Cloud Cable Car each year.

CHOO, CHOO, CHUNNEL!

Want to take a quick visit to France? Hop on a train! You might be asking how that's possible – after all, France and England are separated by a large body of water without a bridge in sight. But you're not going over the water; you're diving under it. The Channel Tunnel, or Chunnel, is an undersea tunnel that connects the south of England with the north of France. Passenger and freight trains – which can transport entire cars – zip through the Chunnel. To get to France from London, it's a quick ride on the Eurostar train from St Pancras International Station or a ride on the Channel Tunnel Rail Link.

IMAGES: IFS Cloud Cable Car at the Royal Docks (above); cars on the Eurotunnel train in the Channel Tunnel (left).

RIDE THE RIVER

The River Thames has been an invaluable part of London since before the city was even London. For thousands of years, people have used the river for trade, communication and – yes – travel!

In the 17th and 18th centuries, the Thames would freeze for months at a time. Locals held 'frost fairs' with shops, games and even camping on the ice.

Today, London river buses include four lines that allow passengers to hop on and off at eight different piers around the city.

Plus, the river buses let you get great views of some of the city's most famous sights, including Tower Bridge (see pages 50–51), the London Eye (see pages 48–49), the Gherkin and much more.

A Thames sightseeing cruise is also lots of fun. On these rides, visitors can have snacks or even a fancy afternoon tea on the water. Sightseeing ahoy!

IMAGE: London and the Thames from above.

SUNKEN SHIPS

Boats have been sailing the waters of the Thames for many centuries – and some even sank in its depths. One of the most famous wrecks is that of the English warship *London*, which sank in 1655 after an accidental explosion. It remained lost in its watery grave in the Thames Estuary until it was rediscovered in 2005.

PLACES TO PLAY

IMAGE: The Hogwarts Express at the Warner Bros Studio Tour London: The Making of Harry Potter.

GET HANDS-ON

SUPER SCIENCE

For any curious kid – or adult! – London's **Science Museum** is an absolute must. You won't want to leave this museum, which has seven floors packed full of interactive exhibits and activities. Fly a space shuttle in a flight simulator, learn the science of video games (while you *play* video games), make interactive art and that's just the start!

The Science Museum has a free app called Treasure Hunters that leads visitors on a search for lesser-known items inside the museum.

THINGS THAT GO

At the **London Transport Museum**, you can do more than learn about historic cars, trains and buses – you can climb aboard! You'll also find unusual rides from the past, like a horse-and-carriage-drawn bus, an underground steam engine and old-fashioned double-decker buses. You'll also find toy cars, posters and so many other transport-themed items.

IMAGES: Space travel exhibit at the Science Museum (above); historic double-decker buses at the London Transport Museum (left); historic costumes at the Young V&A (opposite top); inside the Horniman Museum (opposite bottom).

PLAYTIME

Lots of museums are dedicated to art, science and ancient history. But there are also some that collect toys! At the **Young V&A**, check out exhibits and collections all about different kinds of playthings, from manga and comic books to dolls, action figurines and puppets. You can also get hands-on to create art and experiments yourself.

SOMETHING FOR EVERYONE

There's loads to see inside the **Horniman Museum & Gardens**: animal taxidermy, musical instruments from around the world, a historic aquarium and even sprawling gardens. But there's also lots to touch! You can go to arts-and-crafts workshops, get up close to animals at the Animal Walk, or feel real museum objects in the hands-on zone.

In the Horniman Butterfly House, visitors can walk among butterflies and moths.

PRIME PARKS

Located in Wiltshire, about 148 km (90 miles) from London, Britain's largest maze can take up to an hour and a half to complete!

DINOSAUR DELIGHT

Looking for adventure? **Crystal Palace Park** is the right place. Here, you'll find large dinosaur sculptures that were erected back in 1854. The grounds also hold a skate park for anyone who wants to hit the pavement, as well as a petting zoo. And if you feel like getting lost? Head for the giant maze first created in 1870!

IMAGES: Prehistoric models at Crystal Palace Park (above); the Diana, Princess of Wales Memorial Playground (opposite top); horseback riding at Lee Valley Regional Park (opposite bottom).

AAARGH!

Get ready to sail the seven seas! Well, not really, but you'll sure feel like you are at the **Diana, Princess of Wales Memorial Playground**. Set off on an 11-km (7-mile) walkway and visit the pirate ship–themed playground. Climb aboard a pirate ship, scale the mast or even walk the plank.

FUN IN THE SUN

At 42 km (26 miles) long, **Lee Valley Regional Park** has all kinds of activities on offer. In warmer weather, white-water rafting is the thing to do, or you can take a boat out on the water for a leisurely ride. No matter the time of year, there's always horseback riding, cycling and even indoor ice-skating. If you're looking for something more low-key, check out the Wildlife Discovery Centre to spot wildlife. The best place to watch the wild? A watchtower where you get all the views!

GAME ON

The town of **Wimbledon** in the London borough of Merton is the home of one of the greatest sports competitions around – the Wimbledon Championships, or All-England Championships. Each year, the world's best tennis players converge at Wimbledon to compete at lawn tennis, a type of tennis played on grass courts.

The Wimbledon Championships have been held for more than 145 years, with the first tournament held in 1877 – making it the oldest tennis tournament in the world. Today's stadium grounds can accommodate 42,000 spectators!

Here, you can pop into the **Wimbledon Lawn Tennis Museum** to learn about the history of the Wimbledon Championships and peek at past trophies. You might also be able to get your hands on one of the yellow tennis balls used at the Championships. They are sometimes sold to fans and the money is given to charity.

Fast Facts

Number of tennis balls used over the course of the Championships: **about 55,000**

Number of cameras needed to film each match: **more than 100**

Early tennis rackets had strings made from animal intestines.

IMAGE: Wimbledon's Centre Court.

38 A Kid's Guide to LONDON

RACKET ROCK STARS

Although only men were allowed to compete at Wimbledon for the first three years, women joined the ranks in 1880 and quickly drew in both players and crowds. Over the years, the game's greatest players have competed at Wimbledon, including Serena Williams, Venus Williams, Billie Jean King, Roger Federer, Steffi Graf and many more.

FOR YOUR AMUSEMENT

THAT'S FUN!

Thorpe Park's Hyperia roller coaster has Europe's tallest inversion – meaning a place on the roller coaster that turns riders upside down!

WILD RIDES

About 32 km (20 miles) southwest of London, you'll find an amusement park jam-packed with more than 30 rides, including looping roller coasters and spine-tingling water rides. Among **Thorpe Park's** rides are Colossus, the world's first roller coaster to include 10 loops and Stealth, the fastest roller coaster in the UK. Need a break? Relax by the pool at Amity Beach.

IMAGES: A roller coaster at Thorpe Park (above); a LEGO re-creation of London at LEGOLAND Windsor Resort (opposite top); a water ride at Chessington World of Adventures Resort (opposite bottom).

LET'S GO LEGO!

Love LEGO or building blocks? Then you'll want to head about an hour outside of London to **LEGOLAND Windsor Resort**, where LEGO-themed rides and activities await. The amusement park is divided into 11 themed lands with more than 55 rides and attractions. Check out Miniland, where you can see LEGO models of sights from around the world. Swing on a giant pirate ship at Pirate Shores, or board a LEGO dragon on a roller coaster in Knight's Kingdom.

Together, Miniland's models – which include Buckingham Palace and the London Eye – were made using 40 million LEGO bricks.

WORLD OF ADVENTURES

Want to get wild? Take a short trip – about an hour – outside of London to **Chessington World of Adventures Resort**. This amusement park and zoo is home to more than 40 thrilling rides and over 1,000 animals from around the world. But one of the most unique attractions might just be the Burnt Stub Mansion – it was built in 1348, making the mansion more than 675 years old! By the 17th century, it was used as a tavern, where travellers would stop to eat and rest.

FAME AWAITS

A WORLD OF WIZARDS

Calling all Potterheads: if you've ever wanted to get a behind-the-scenes view into the world of Harry Potter, now's your chance. At **Warner Bros. Studio Tour London: The Making of *Harry Potter***, guests will have a chance to explore the movie series like never before. Visitors can enter the magic by stepping into the actual sets used in the films, from the Great Hall to Diagon Alley to the Forbidden Forest! You'll also see props and costumes used in the films and even get to peek at special effects that make movie magic.

Fast Facts

Number of prop coins made for the Harry Potter films: **more than 210,000**

Number of life-size animatronic Buckbeaks made: **3**

Number of wand boxes made: **17,000**

WONDER WALL
Visitors to King's Cross Station can spy Platform 9 ¾, where a 'disappearing' trolley cart is in the wall.

University College London was used as a location to film several films, such as Batman Begins and The Dark Knight.

MOVIE MAGIC

The *Harry Potter* films are far from the only movies filmed in London. If you're a fan of Paddington Bear, be sure to check out locations around town like **Paddington Station**, the railway station for which the little bear is named, or Regent's Canal in Camden, where Paddington famously rode a dog. Film fans and booklovers can also search out other famous sights and monuments around the city. Check out the statue of Peter Pan in Kensington Gardens, or famed *Mary Poppins* locations including St Paul's Cathedral (see pages 76–77) or the Bank of England.

IMAGES: Warner Bros. Studio Tour London: The Making of *Harry Potter* (above); a statue of Paddington Bear inside Paddington Station (left).

Places to Play 43

SHOWTIME!

For much of the 17th century in England, only men were allowed to act in plays.

PLAYS FROM THE PAST

Even more than four centuries after he lived, William Shakespeare remains one of the most famous playwrights in the world. Visit **Shakespeare's Globe Theatre** to watch how a Shakespeare play would have been performed in the 17th century. The first Globe Theatre opened in 1599. Today's Globe Theatre is a reconstruction built near the original site in 1997. Like the original, it has a semi-open roof and circular audience stands. Actors often wear costumes that mimic the clothing that was worn in the 17th-century plays.

IMAGES: Shakespeare's Globe Theatre (above); Puppet Theatre Barge (opposite top); Royal Opera House (opposite bottom).

PUPPET PLAYS

For this venue, you'll be heading to Regent's Canal. That's right – this performance is on the water! Since 1978, the **Puppet Theatre Barge** has been performing puppet shows on a barge, or flat-bottomed boat. Audiences climb aboard and descend below deck to watch intricate string puppets, or marionettes, act out stories and songs.

A ROYAL TIME

Set among the West End's many theatres, the historic **Royal Opera House** was first home to the Covent Garden Theatre, which opened in 1732. The building burned down twice – once in 1808 and again in 1856, when firelight was used to light the indoors. Luckily, the house was rebuilt again and reopened in 1858. During World War I, the opera house closed and was used to store furniture. In World War II, it became a dance hall. Today, the fancy grand theatre is home to all kinds of musical performances, including operas, choruses and ballets. You can even take a behind-the-scenes tour!

Places to Play 45

WHAT A VIEW!

IMAGE: The London Eye.

SLIDE AND RIDE

GET AN EYEFUL

What's better than getting an awesome view of the city? Enjoying a ride while you do it! Hop on the **London Eye**, an enormous Ferris wheel on the banks of the Thames, to look out over all of London. Built in 1999, the London Eye is one of the world's tallest Ferris wheels. Afraid of heights? Not to worry – the giant wheel has enclosed carriages with enough room for several people to stand or sit. (This also makes it rainy day-friendly!) Once you're up high, you'll get panoramic views of the city.

Before the London Eye, the city had the Great Wheel: a 94-m-tall (308 ft) Ferris wheel that was built in 1895.

The slide is made of enough steel to build 265 double-decker buses.

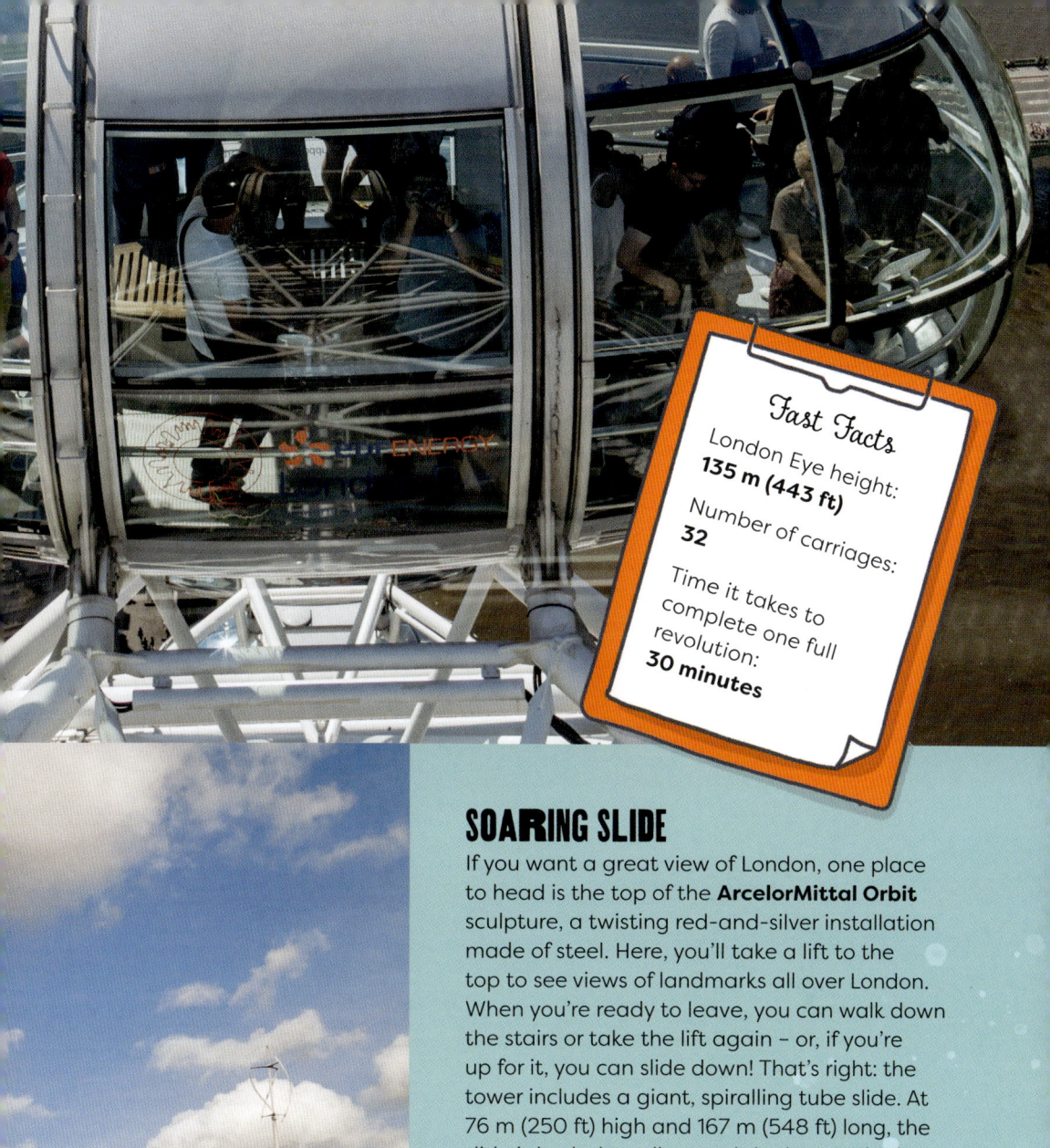

Fast Facts

London Eye height:
135 m (443 ft)

Number of carriages:
32

Time it takes to complete one full revolution:
30 minutes

SOARING SLIDE

If you want a great view of London, one place to head is the top of the **ArcelorMittal Orbit** sculpture, a twisting red-and-silver installation made of steel. Here, you'll take a lift to the top to see views of landmarks all over London. When you're ready to leave, you can walk down the stairs or take the lift again – or, if you're up for it, you can slide down! That's right: the tower includes a giant, spiralling tube slide. At 76 m (250 ft) high and 167 m (548 ft) long, the slide is both the tallest and the longest in the world. Riders zip along at up to 24 km/h (15 mph), getting glimpses of London as they go.

IMAGES: London Eye passenger capsule (above); ArcelorMittal Orbit (left).

A TOWERING BRIDGE

With its castle-like towers, enormous drawbridge and sweeping structural supports, this bridge is one of the most iconic landmarks in London. Because of that, many people think that this is London Bridge. In reality, this is **Tower Bridge**! Tower Bridge was built from 1886 to 1894 and styled to blend in with the older parts of London.

Today, Tower Bridge is one of the most famous views in the city. Catch sight of this icon from the banks of the Thames, or from other viewing spots like the London Eye (see pages 48–49) or the Shard (see page 54). If you prefer, you can get a peep at the rest of the city from Tower Bridge's famous, well, towers. Visitors can climb up and walk along a glass walkway that connects the two towers. While you're on the bridge enjoying the views of the city, don't forget to peek below your feet – through the glass floor!

Fast Facts
Years it took to build: **8**

Time it takes to raise the bascules: **1 minute**

How often the bridge raises: **about 800 times a year, or twice a day on average**

IMAGE: Tower Bridge raises its bascules for a ship.

Just 0.8 km (0.5 miles) away from Tower Bridge is London Bridge. The original structure collapsed, leading to the famous nursery rhyme we know today.

AN ENGINEERING FEAT
One of the biggest challenges facing the engineers of Tower Bridge was how to create a bridge that would span the Thames and allow people to cross, but also allow boats and ships to continue down the river freely. The solution was to create a bascule bridge: a type of road made from two parts that join in the middle and can lift up from either side to let boats pass.

ENTER THE ARENA

SCALE THE TOP

Thrill-seekers hoping for a view that also gets the heart pumping need look no further. Visitors to the **O2 Arena** can book a guided climb up the arena's domed roof. That's right – climbers can strap on a harness and then scale the building to its 52-m (170-ft) peak. At the top, you'll be able to take in 360-degree views of everything around you. Making the climb at sunset or in the evening to see the city lights is extra special. There's even an option to enjoy a meal at the top!

Fast Facts

O2 Arena capacity: **20,000 people**

Number of tickets sold in 2023: **2.5 million**

Number of tower 'spikes': **12**

London's Tottenham Hotspur Stadium also offers a daredevil climb – only this one is over a glass walkway.

ROCK ON

Packed with world-renowned acts, the O2 Arena is considered one of the busiest arenas in the world thanks to the incredible number of tickets it sells. If you want an up-close view of musicians, orchestras, comedians or sports competitions, this is the place to be. First opened in 2000 as the Millennium Dome before reopening in 2007, the arena is almost as famous for its spiky domed roof as it is for its shows, which have featured Céline Dion, Lizzo, the Jonas Brothers and other famous musicians. More than an arena, the O2 has bowling, restaurants, an enormous mall and even giant trampolines!

IMAGES: O2 Arena roof (above); Jonas Brothers at the O2 Arena (left).

FAMOUS LOOKOUTS

The Shard's high-speed lift can ascend 68 floors in just one minute.

PYRAMID PINNACLE

A modern marvel, the **Shard** is a shimmering glass pyramid that towers over the city: at 309.6 m (1,016 ft), the skyscraper is not just the tallest building in England, but in all of western Europe. It also offers some of the greatest views. Head up to the 69th floor to the main viewing platform and check out the view. From the platform, you can see up to 64 km (40 miles) away! Then take things farther by travelling up to the tippy-top: on the 72nd floor, you can scope things out from the sky-high open-air platform.

IMAGES: The Shard (above); Piccadilly Circus (opposite top); inside Covent Garden Market (opposite bottom).

SEE THE CIRCUS

Okay, so it's not *really* a circus – but London's **Piccadilly Circus** is still one of the best places to sit back and observe the hubbub of the city. Built in 1819, Piccadilly Circus is often referred to as a miniature Times Square (as in the bustling Times Square of New York City). It's always buzzing with people, traffic and enormous neon billboards. Piccadilly is also home to a fully underground theatre! Grab a seat by the fountain with the statue of Eros and do some prime people-watching.

> Cups were once chained to the Piccadilly Circus fountain's base so people could drink the water, but they were stolen quickly after they were installed.

MARKET FUN

Just as Piccadilly Circus isn't actually a circus, **Covent Garden** is not really a garden. Instead, this historic area is packed full of fun things to see and do. The site's history goes back to 1630 – that's almost 400 years! Back then it was a public square. In 1828, the Covent Garden Market Building opened, eventually becoming a busy place for shopping, eating and having fun! See if you can spot jugglers, acrobats, or other street performers outside the market building, or catch a concert inside the market while you enjoy a bite.

AWESOME ART

TOP OF THE BUNCH

The **Tate Modern** is one of the most-visited museums in the world and it's housed inside a former power station. The station is made of 4.2 million bricks and has a huge chimney. Inside the museum are six escalators and nine lifts to get visitors where they want to go. The modern and contemporary art comes from across the globe and there are interactive art pieces and giant installations, too. You'll find art by Pablo Picasso, Yayoi Kusama, Andy Warhol and many more. For a fantastic view, the top of the museum's Blavatnik Building is the place to be.

FIRST THINGS FIRST

The South Kensington Museum had plenty of world firsts. It was the first museum to use gas lighting in its galleries, the first museum to collect photographs as art and the first to open a public restaurant.

Fast Facts

Height of the Tate Modern's chimney: **99 m (325 ft)**

Number of annual visitors: **more than 3 million**

Number of floors in Blavatnik Building: **10**

MUSEUM MARVELS

First founded in 1852 as the South Kensington Museum, the **Victoria and Albert Museum** (also known as the V&A) is the largest art museum in London – and the eighth largest in the world. As the South Kensington, it was the first museum in the world to have gas lights in the gallery. This allowed the museum to open at night, before electricity was invented. In 1857, the museum moved to its current location with grand architecture inside and out. Inside are more than 2.8 million objects, so there's something for everyone, from fashion to paintings to sculptures to ancient ceramics.

IMAGES: Tate Modern (above); costumes from the **Christian Dior: Designer of Dreams** *exhibition at the Victoria and Albert Museum (left).*

LET'S EAT!

IMAGE: *Eton mess dessert.*

TIME FOR TEA

Today, tea is a common drink around the world – and the British have taken it even further by perfecting afternoon tea. While it can take many forms, the traditional tea menu often includes a type of British baked good called a scone. Bread-like and slightly sweet, scones are often served with jam and a thick cream known as clotted cream. Also popular are small, crustless finger sandwiches (called such because you eat them with your hands).

To take part in this classic London tradition, step back in time at **Twinings**, the oldest tea shop in London. Twinings has been around for more than 300 years! Themed tea parties are also held around town. They are designed to make it feel like you have stepped into a fantasy world. Sip tea with the Mad Hatter at an *Alice in Wonderland* party, nosh on treats at a *Charlie and the Chocolate Factory* tea time, or explore your magical side with a Harry Potter-themed tea!

Some companies hold tea tours on double-decker buses that cruise the city while you sip.

IMAGE: A traditional tea featuring tea, finger sandwiches and pastries.

COMPLETELY CLASSIC

ORDER UP!

There's nothing quite as classic as a full English breakfast, also known as a fry-up. Centuries ago, English breakfasts likely included roasted pigeons, sheep tongues and broiled kidneys! Today, diners dig in to sausage, bacon, fried eggs, baked beans, mushrooms, tomatoes, toast and even black pudding (see page 67).

FRY FEAST

In the 17th century, Jewish immigrants brought a unique way of preparing fish to England: frying it in a crispy, flour-based batter. Then, 200 years later, French fries – or chips, as they are called in England – started to become popular, too. At some point, the two started being served together and the first ever fish and chips store opened in 1860. Today, fish and chips are so popular in the UK that more than 1.6 million tonnes (1.7 million tons) of potatoes are made into fries every year – that's the same weight as over 4,000 jumbo jets!

SWELL WELLINGTON

No one is certain who first invented the beef Wellington. It could have been named after the duke of Wellington, who was also a British general. Another theory? It was named after an old boot known as the Wellington boot – because the dish kind of looks like one when cooked! Either way, the beef fillet coated in chopped mushrooms and liver and wrapped inside a puff pastry is an iconic dish in England.

IMAGES: A full English breakfast (opposite top); fish and chips (opposite bottom); beef Wellington (left); Yorkshire pudding (below).

FULL OF FLAVOUR

Historians think that in the 17th century, Yorkshire puddings were cooked beneath roasting meat to catch the drippings. Today, the fluffy, savoury and golden delights are a delicious addition to a classic roast dinner, often served with gravy. They are so popular that there was once an annual Yorkshire Pudding Boat Race. Participants had to build a Yorkshire pudding boat they could fit in and take out on the water!

In the UK the first Sunday of February is National Yorkshire Pudding Day.

FOOD FUSION

Chicken tikka masala is a popular dish in restaurants around the world. This rich curry dish consists of chicken that's been roasted in a special type of oven known as a tandoor. It is then served in a spiced tomato and cream sauce.

No one knows for sure who first created chicken tikka masala. Some historians believe it originated as a dish in Pakistan and northern India. However, most historians believe that the meal was created in Scotland (part of Great Britain) when a Pakistani chef adapted a curry to British tastes by making it creamier and less spicy. Today, chicken tikka masala remains one of the most popular dishes across Britain, along with other Southeast Asian foods. In fact, London's Brick Lane is known for its many delicious Indian restaurants that line the street.

Chicken tikka masala is sometimes considered one of Britain's national dishes.

IMAGE: Chicken tikka masala with spices and naan.

GLOBAL GRUB
Southeast Asia is not the only region to influence England in its popular dishes. You can also find Caribbean cuisine, such as jerk chicken or curried goat. British-Chinese cuisine is popular, too: fried rice dishes tend to come with curries, or you can try chow mein and chips!

UNEXPECTED EATS

FEELING JELLY?

This dish might strike you as a bit unusual, but jellied eels are actually traditional! Back in the 1700s, many Londoners ate eels as cheap but filling meals. Easily available in the Thames, these fish offered lots of protein and were tasty. One way to make the meal last was to turn it into a savoury jelly, or an aspic. The eels were boiled and flavoured with vinegar and seasonings. As the dish cooled, it solidified into a wiggly jelly. But it's not just a thing of the past; the meal is still popular.

IMAGES: Jellied eels (above); a traditional breakfast featuring black pudding (opposite top); stargazy pie (opposite bottom).

PECULIAR PUDDING

Before you dig in, let it be known: this thick pudding isn't a dessert. Although 'pudding' is often used to refer to desserts in Britain (see page 68), it can also mean a savoury dish. Black pudding is a type of sausage made from both the meat and blood of an animal, often a pig. The blood is usually first cooked with a filler, such as oatmeal, so it will thicken as it cools. Eaten since at least the 15th century, it is described as having a meaty, nutty and sometimes even slightly metallic taste.

According to legend, stargazy pie was first created to honour a 16th-century hero named Tom Bawcock who helped end a famine in his Cornish village with a trove of fish.

PIECE OF PIE

If you were served a piece of stargazy pie without warning, it might be a bit . . . startling. That's because the savoury pie comes with several fish heads poking out of the top, gazing starward. This surprising-looking historic dish originated in Cornwall and has become hard to find today. But don't worry: you can still get your hands on it at certain times of the year. Stargazy pie has been known to pop up in several shops across London during British Pie Week, which takes place in early March.

Let's Eat! 67

SWEET TREATS

PLENTY OF PUDDINGS

Unlike in the case of Yorkshire pudding and black pudding, the word 'pudding' in Britain usually refers to a dessert. Be sure to check out some of the most popular puddings as you make your way around town. Sticky toffee pudding is just like it sounds: this cake is made with sticky dates and smothered in toffee sauce. Similarly, banoffee pie is named for its two main ingredients: bananas and toffee. If those don't take your fancy, how about an Eton mess? This dish includes layers of meringue, whipped cream and strawberries. Yum!

A British dessert called Christmas pudding – containing dried fruits and spices – is set on fire right before it is served!

BISCUITS FROM A QUEEN

According to lore, Queen Elizabeth I helped invent the gingerbread man when she ordered gingerbread cookies to be made to look like visitors to her court and then given as gifts.

BISCUITS FOR DESSERT

How about some biscuits? The word 'biscuit' comes from the French words for 'twice cooked'. These sweet treats are delicious, and there are so many to choose from! Scottish shortbreads are buttery and crumbly; chocolate digestives are semi-sweet and glazed in chocolate. And then there's the oaty Hobnob - which, according to some studies, is one of the best biscuits for dunking in cups of tea. Dunking is a popular tradition that makes the tasty treat softer, and it can even sweeten up your tea! You can find biscuits in supermarkets and specialty stores all across London. See how many different kinds you can sample, and just try to pick a favourite!

IMAGES: Banoffee pie (above); shortbread biscuits (left).

ALONG THE THAMES

IMAGE: Crossing the Thames on the Millennium Bridge.

TALK OF THE THAMES

In 1014, English king Ethelred reclaimed London from Viking invasions by sailing up the Thames to defeat them.

A WONDERFUL WATERWAY

The Thames was running through the heart of London before the city even existed. The first official site of London – then called Londinium – got its start 2,000 years ago when ancient Romans sailed up the river. Over the centuries, rulers – such as King Athelstan, the first king of England and William the Conqueror, an invading ruler originally from northern France – established important sites along the riverbanks. In the 17th century, the Thames also became a very important route for merchants and traders carrying goods. Nowadays, some of the city's greatest sights are here.

IMAGES: An illustration of a Roman ship in Londinium (above); swans in the Thames (opposite top); an 1859 cartoon featuring the figure of 'Father Thames' (opposite bottom).

COOL CREATURES

Despite being in the middle of a city, the Thames is home to some incredible wildlife. On top of many species of fish – including European eels, flounder, mullet and more – there are plenty of birds and marine mammals that make the Thames their home. Keep your eyes peeled and you might spot geese, swans, herons and even circling peregrine falcons. If you're lucky, you might get a glimpse of harbour seals, grey seals, or even porpoises and bottlenose dolphins!

In other parts of the country, the Thames Estuary is home to many more animals, including short-snouted seahorses, otters and at least five species of shark.

A STINKY SITUATION

Today, conservationists and government officials make many efforts to help keep the Thames clean and full of life. But it wasn't always this way. For much of history, people tossed their rubbish – including their sewage – directly into the river. Over time, as the population grew, this became a bigger and bigger problem. By 1858, the water became so foul and polluted that it could be smelled throughout the city – and many members of the nearby Parliament even left London because of it! This became known as the Great Stink of London. Luckily, it inspired officials to take action and clean the water.

Along the Thames

MORE THAN A TOWER

AN ANCIENT FORT

The **Tower of London** is actually a concentric castle: it consists of several rings of defences within each other. From start to finish, it took 20 years to complete! It got its start in the 1070s – more than 900 years ago – when William the Conqueror ordered a fortress built along the Thames. Over time, it has been used as a fortress, a palace and a prison!

ROYAL RESIDENCES

Over the centuries, the Tower of London became more than a simple fortress. In the 13th century under Henry III, the castle was transformed into a royal palace, including residences, a great hall, kitchens and more. It even became home to the Royal Menagerie – a private royal zoo (see page 99)! On top of that, the tower was further expanded to hold an armoury and a coin mint where coins were made.

IMAGES: Outside the Tower of London (above); King Edward I's bedchamber in the Tower of London (left); a portrait of Anne Boleyn, Henry VIII's second wife (opposite top); the Imperial State Crown (opposite bottom).

SPOOKY STORIES

In addition to its impressive past, the tower also has a more gruesome history: it served as a prison and execution site and even included a torture chamber. According to legend, some guests have reported seeing the ghostly figures of those who met their untimely ends at the tower. One famous ghost sighting is that of Henry VIII's second wife Anne Boleyn, who was beheaded at the tower.

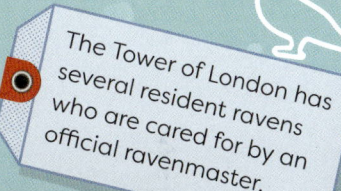

The Tower of London has several resident ravens who are cared for by an official ravenmaster.

TOWER TOURS

It might surprise you to know that the Tower of London has been open to visitors since the 1700s. Today, more than three million people visit each year to discover what life might have been like at the tower through the centuries. Visitors can watch reenactments, check out ancient weapons and even peek at the sparkly Crown Jewels – the Tower is used to protect treasures that have belonged to England's monarchs.

SEE ST PAUL'S CATHEDRAL

The history of **St Paul's Cathedral** goes back to before the building we see today. The first known structure was a cathedral dedicated to the Christian St Paul in 604. After it burned down, another was built – only to be sacked by Vikings in 962. A third cathedral, built in 1087, also burned! In the late 1100s, a fourth cathedral – known as Old St Paul's – was built. This stood for nearly 500 years and may have still been standing if it weren't for a tragedy that befell the city in 1666: the Great Fire of London.

Work on a new St Paul's began in 1668. This cathedral included the dome that still dots the London skyline. It's one of the largest domes in the world. Visitors can head to the top where an observation platfrom – the Golden Gallery – is the perfect place for a great view. There's also a Whispering Gallery. What's that? A circular walkway halfway up the dome where something whispered on one wall can be heard against another wall 34 m (112 ft) away!

> The final resting place of Sir Alexander Fleming, the physicist who discovered penicillin, is at St Paul's Cathedral.

IMAGE: St Paul's Cathedral.

Fast Facts

Height of the tallest part of St Paul's: **111 m (365 ft)**

Number of steps to reach the dome: **530**

Number of monuments in St Paul's: **around 500**

THE GREAT FIRE

On 2 September 1666, a fire accidentally started in a bakery near London Bridge. At the time, many of the structures in London were made of wood. This meant that the fire spread quickly, burning out of control and destroying more than half the city – including Old St Paul's – in its blaze.

TOUR TRAFALGAR SQUARE

A STABLE SPOT

Before it was the open plaza you see today, **Trafalgar Square** was the Royal Mews, or horse stables. These were moved in the early 1800s to Buckingham Palace (see pages 86-87) and the area became a plaza. Nelson's Column, a huge monument that stands tall over the square, was built to honour British admiral Horatio Nelson's 1805 victory at the Battle of Trafalgar. The monument is 56 m (185 ft) tall. That's as high as 18.5 basketball hoops stacked end to end!

LION KINGS

Among the most visited attractions in Trafalgar Square are its four lions – not real lions, but larger-than-life statues made of bronze. Located at the base of Nelson's Column, these large lions were erected in honour of Admiral Nelson. Today, the felines stand guard at the column and sit in a perfect place for a picture.

The four lions are the subject of interesting lore: it is said that if Big Ben (see pages 80-81) ever chimes 13 times, the lions will come to life.

SPLASHY SCULPTURES

Mermaids, dolphins and sharks in the city! The Trafalgar Square fountains feature creatures of the sea, looking like they're about to dive right into the blue waters. These fountains were first built in 1845 as a way to take up space and prevent people from gathering to protest the government. In the 1930s, they were redesigned and given decorative additions. The fountains are a must-see after dark, when they light up the night!

Trafalgar Square was once home to what many call London's smallest police station, a lookout box carved into a hollow lamppost. About the size of a closet, it could hold only two prisoners at a time.

TAKE AN ART BREAK

There's not just a lot to see in Trafalgar Square; there's so much around it, too. At the nearby **National Portrait Gallery**, you'll find more than 1,000 portraits, including paintings, photographs, sculptures and drawings – some dating back more than 1,000 years! In 1856, the gallery brought in its first portrait – of William Shakespeare. It was painted in 1610. The tallest painting? It's 4 m (13 ft) tall. The smallest is the size of a thumbnail!

IMAGES: The fountains at Trafalgar Square (opposite top); a lion statue at Trafalgar Square (opposite bottom); decorative additions in the Trafalgar Square fountains (above); inside the National Portrait Gallery (right).

Along the Thames

POWERHOUSES

THE COOLEST CLOCK

Big Ben is in the running to be perhaps the most iconic landmark in all of London. As part of the Houses of Parliament, the clock tower is nicknamed not for the tower itself – which is actually called Elizabeth Tower – but for the bell inside. When construction for the current Houses of Parliament began in 1837, architects also designed a grand clock tower and enormous bell. However, the bell took a couple tries. The first bell cracked and had to be melted down completely. The second bell also cracked, but was fitted with a lighter hammer and turned so that the unbroken side could be struck. This is the bell that still rings!

Fast Facts

Big Ben bell weight: **13.7 tonnes (15.1 tons)**

Bell height: **2.2 m (7.2 ft)**

Bell diameter: **2.7 m (8.9 ft)**

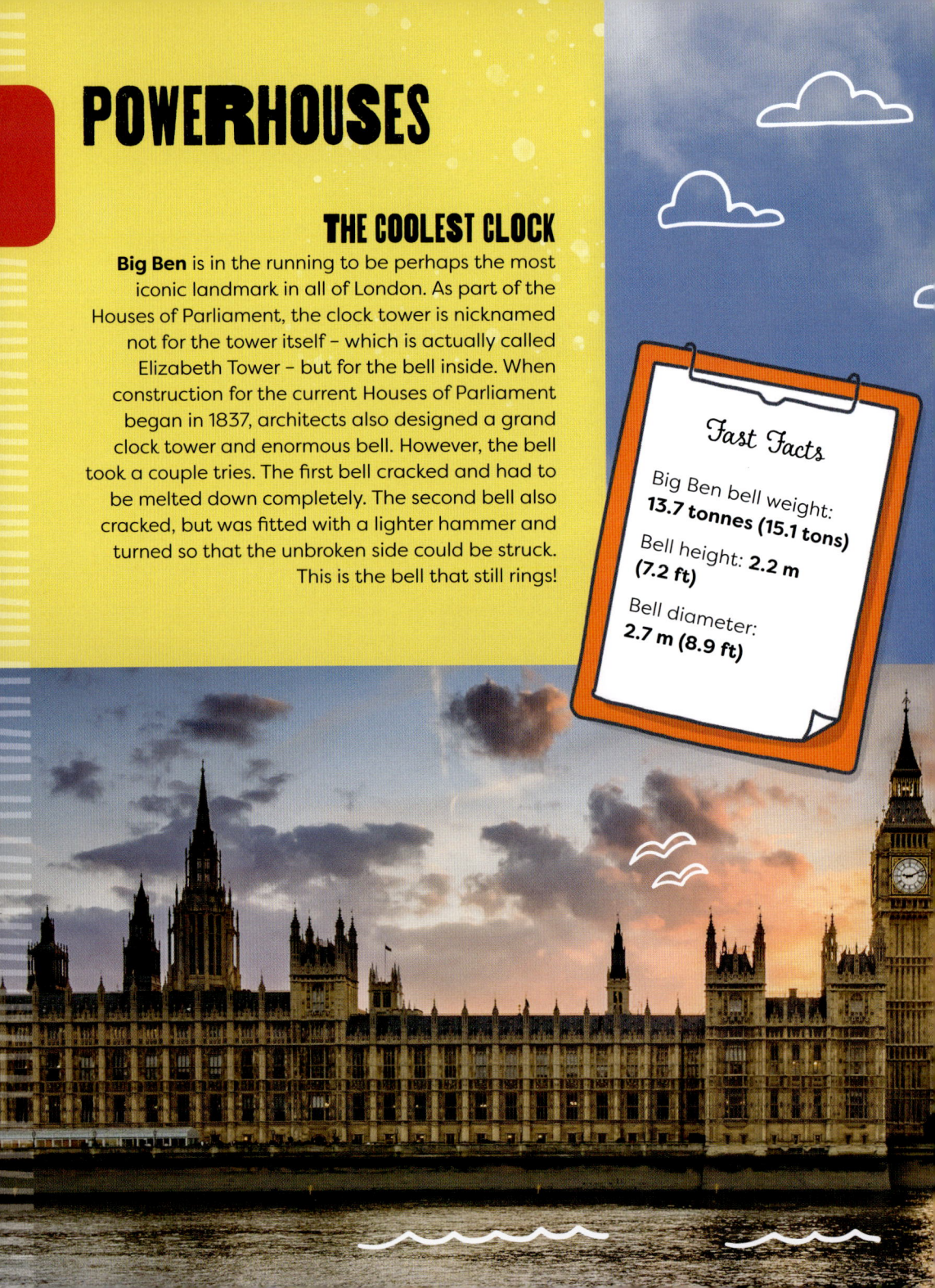

MAKING A GOVERNMENT

In 1295, an early Parliament known as the Model Parliament consisted of the king's advisers and local representatives, such as knights. Over the centuries, Parliament became a governing body (that at times aided or opposed the king). By the 1700s, the power of the monarchy had declined and Parliament became the main governing body.

PEEK AT PARLIAMENT

The Houses of Parliament, officially known as the **Palace of Westminster**, is where the British government meets and works. The palace was first constructed in the 11th century and used as a royal residence for 400 years. In the 1500s, King Edward VI granted his Parliament use of parts of the palace. But it wasn't until 1834, when the entire building was destroyed by a fire, that the version of the Palace of Westminster you now see was built. Today, there are 1,100 rooms, more than 100 staircases and miles of passageways weaving around the building!

IMAGES: Close-up of Big Ben's clock face (above); the Palace of Westminster from across the Thames (left).

Along the Thames 81

SET SAIL

LEARN THE ROPES

Beginning in the 17th century, Britain became one of the world's major maritime powers, at times boasting the largest and most powerful fleets in the world. Its fascinating history is captured right on the Thames at the **National Maritime Museum** where visitors can discover stories of epic ocean exploration, from how sailors navigated the seas using the stars to replicas of ships used hundreds of years ago.

STRIKE GOLD

Get hands-on and explore living history by visiting this awesome historic ship now docked on the Thames. Climb aboard the **Golden Hinde**, a replica of the Elizabethan galleon captained by the legendary British explorer and privateer Sir Francis Drake. Meet character actors dressed in period clothing and learn about life on the ship.

The Golden Hinde was the first British ship to circumnavigate, or sail all the way around, Earth.

ALL HANDS ON DECK

Want to learn more about ocean battles during World War II? Then climb aboard the **HMS** *Belfast*, a warship built in 1936. Visitors can explore the ship's nine decks to discover how the ship's crews ate, lived and fought. A simulator lets guests try their hand at steering the ship and boat enthusiasts can take a seat in the captain's chair.

IMAGES: Outside the National Maritime Museum (opposite top); replica of the Golden Hinde (opposite bottom); HMS Belfast in front of Tower Bridge (left); Cutty Sark (below).

> A privateer was a type of government-approved pirate who was given the go-ahead to attack enemy trading ships.

SAIL AWAY

If sailing's more your speed, then avast ye landlubbers: the **Cutty Sark** is a 19th-century tea clipper, a sailing ship designed to speed through waters and haul traded goods (like tea). Today, visitors will meet actors dressed as historical characters, as well as be able to play interactive games while exploring the ship. You can even get a rare view by walking beneath the ship to check out its unique copper hull.

> The Cutty Sark's maiden voyage took the ship from London to Shanghai, China, in 1870.

THE ROYAL TREATMENT

IMAGE: The Queen's Birthday Parade outside Buckingham Palace.

FIT FOR A KING

Buckingham Palace has 775 rooms (including 78 bathrooms)!

BUCKINGHAM BASICS

London has plenty of palaces (see pages 90–91), but **Buckingham Palace** is *the* palace: it has served as the royal residence of queens and kings since the early 1820s, when King George IV had an existing mansion converted into a palace. It is also the place where many national celebrations and royal ceremonies take place. During certain times of the year, visitors can tour 19 public rooms (including the Throne Room) and peek at treasures from the Royal Collection, such as a grand piano covered in gold, paintings by famed artists, or throne chairs, including the one made for Queen Victoria in 1837.

IMAGES: Buckingham Palace (above); a royal coronation coach in the Royal Mews (opposite top); part of the Changing of the Guard ceremony at Buckingham Palace (opposite bottom).

NEXT-DOOR NEIGHBOURS

Gallop on over to the **Royal Mews**, or the royal stables. These stables were established in 1825, but existed in what is now Trafalgar Square for more than four centuries before that. Today, the Royal Mews have expanded to include all of the royal methods of transportation, from horse-drawn carriages to cars. A standout is the Gold State Coach, a carriage that has been used for more than 260 years and is covered in real gold.

The Foot Guards have worn the same tall, fluffy bearskin hats for more than 200 years.

SOLDIER SWAP

One of the most famous things to do while at Buckingham Palace is to watch the Changing of the Guard. Since the 1600s, soldiers known as Foot Guards have stood watch over the royal residences. The Changing of the Guard, also known as Guard Mounting, is a ceremony during which the current on-duty soldiers (called the Old Guard) are replaced with a new group (the New Guard). Visitors can watch the ceremony, which takes place several times a week and lasts for about 45 minutes.

Traditionally, the King's Guard is expected to remain very still and avoid smiling, laughing or talking.

The Royal Treatment

ASTOUNDING ABBEY

Westminster Abbey is the site of England's coronations, the ceremony that crowns a new ruler. It is also the location for many national ceremonies, including royal weddings.

Westminster Abbey's first official coronation was that of William I, also known as William the Conqueror, a king who shaped England's history. William I was a duke of Normandy, an area of northern France. In 1066, he invaded England, conquering the Saxons who lived there. He was crowned king of England on Christmas Day of that year.

If you look way up high in the nave, you'll see the 'Door to Heaven,' an actual door that leads to the roof of the Abbey. It is under this door that a new monarch is crowned.

Among all the grandeur of the Abbey sits something very simple – Britain's oldest door. Used as an entry to the Chapter House, the wood for the door was likely felled after 1032. The door itself was crafted in the 1050s, making it almost 1,000 years old.

IMAGE: The funeral of Queen Elizabeth II at Westminster Abbey.

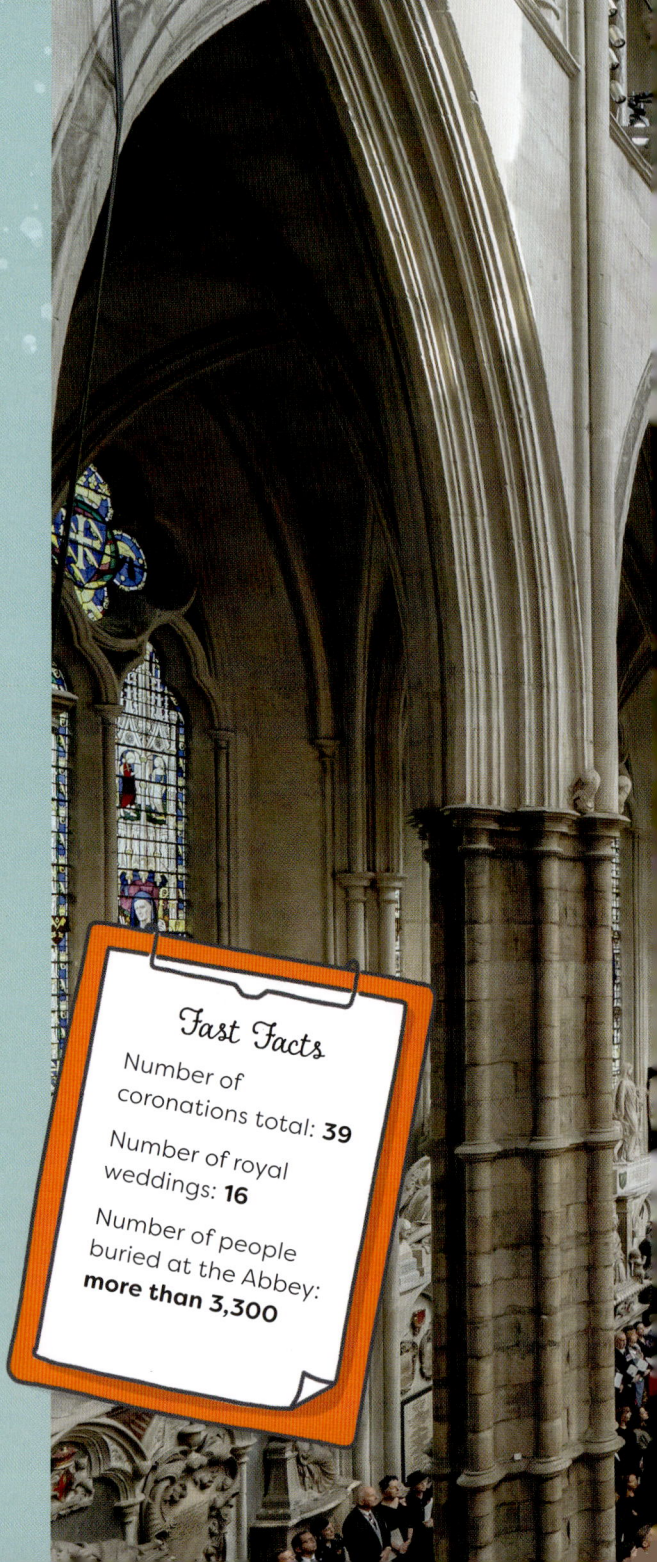

Fast Facts

Number of coronations total: **39**

Number of royal weddings: **16**

Number of people buried at the Abbey: **more than 3,300**

POET'S CORNER

Many famous people are buried at Westminster Abbey, including renowned poets and authors, such as Geoffrey Chaucer, William Shakespeare (see page 44), Jane Austen and Charles Dickens – and composers, such as George Frideric Handel.

THESE RESIDENCES RULE!

WIND DOWN IN WINDSOR

Just an hour car or train ride from the city, **Windsor Castle** has been a historic royal residence for more than 900 years. Established by William the Conqueror (see page 88), it was built as one of nine defensive castles that formed a ring around London. The castle is home to the oldest continually working kitchen in the country – it's been running for more than 650 years!

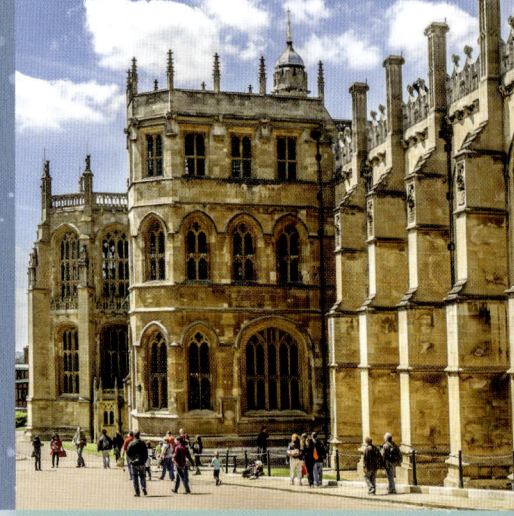

Many royal weddings have been held in St George's Chapel at Windsor Castle, including Prince Harry and Meghan, the Duke and Duchess of Sussex, in 2018.

KENSINGTON DIGS

Built in the 17th century, **Kensington Palace** started as a small villa. It was Queen Mary II who transformed it into a palace. Queen Mary II and her husband King William III used their new lavish home to host grand balls. Later, King George I commissioned paintings on what is now called the King's Staircase. The art includes life-size depictions of members of his court. Today, it is home to William and Kate, Prince and Princess of Wales.

The Jewel Room is home to a stunning emerald tiara – a gift from Prince Albert to Queen Victoria in 1845.

HISTORIC HAMPTON COURT

Unlike other royal residences, no one lives at **Hampton Court Palace** – at least, not anymore. This grand estate was built in the early 1500s for King Henry VIII and also housed other members of the House of Tudor dynasty, such as Elizabeth I. On top of the historic great hall and kitchens, Hampton Court is famous for its hedge maze, which is the oldest in the country.

An annual tulip festival is held at Hampton Court Palace.

THAT'S MY KEW!

Kew Palace was built in the 17th century for a London silk merchant. The stately red mansion within the well-manicured grounds of **Kew Gardens** later became a summer home for King George III and Queen Charlotte and their family. Swans, buffalo, kangaroos and even quaggas – a now extinct zebra-like animal – once wandered the grounds of Kew Palace, near Queen Charlotte's cottage. The kangaroos were the first in Britain.

IMAGES: St George's Chapel at Windsor Castle (opposite top); Kensington Palace and Gardens (opposite bottom); hedge maze at Hampton Court (above); Kew Gardens (right).

MAJESTIC MUSEUMS

KING'S BLING

Located at Buckingham Palace (see pages 86-87), the **King's Gallery** (formerly the Queen's Gallery) is a marvellous museum that features items from the Royal Collection, which includes more than one million items belonging to the British monarchs of the past 500 years. Despite its glittering contents, this collection came from some rather disturbing beginnings. In the 17th century, England was plagued by a series of civil wars between King Charles I and Parliament. King Charles I was executed in 1649 and much of the royal holdings were sold. When the monarchy was reinstituted in 1660, the Royal Collection was formed.

King George III bought a portrait of the Royal Academy's founders for 500 guineas, or the equivalent of about £65,000.

> At the King's Gallery gift shop, visitors can buy stuffed animal versions of the late Queen Elizabeth II's corgis.

BACK TO SCHOOL

The **Royal Academy of Arts** was founded in 1768 by King George III and a group of 36 artists and architects as a school and a gallery – and it remains so today. It is the oldest art school in Britain. Here, you'll see art of all kinds, from sculptures to photography to paintings to amazing architecture. With more than 46,000 items in its collection, there's a whole lot to explore. The Royal Academy of Arts is also home to *Taddei Tondo*, the only marble sculpture in the UK created by the famous Italian artist and sculptor Michelangelo.

IMAGES: The King's Gallery at Buckingham Palace (above); Royal Academy of Arts (left).

GARDENS GALORE

NOBLE NATURE

Green Park – linking Hyde Park and St James's Park – was created by King Charles II in 1660 so he could take his daily walks. For centuries, royals in London have been spending time enjoying natural spaces. Today, many of these royal grounds have been turned into public parks, officially known as the **Royal Parks**. In addition to Green Park, there are seven other Royal Parks in London. One is actually Brompton Cemetery, which is not only a place where some notable people are buried, but also home to subterranean catacombs closed off by cast-iron doors with snake carvings.

IMAGES: Green Park (above); St James's Park (opposite top); Kensington Gardens (opposite bottom).

From Hunting to Hangout

Located near three royal palaces, **St James's Park** is London's oldest Royal Park. The park was created in 1532 by King Henry VIII, who wanted (another) deer park for his hunts. The park also became a prime place for festivals, parties and even jousting competitions. Now the grounds are known for their peace and quiet – at least when there isn't a royal ceremony in progress. Be sure to keep your eyes peeled for the pelicans that have called the park home since 1664.

Beautiful Blooms

Created by Queen Caroline in the 18th century, **Kensington Gardens** are known for their outstanding beauty. With sweeping, historic trees framing brightly coloured flower beds and fancy fountains, it's no surprise that these grounds were once part of Kensington Palace (see page 90). The park is home to fields of wildflowers, as well as wildlife like birds, squirrels and foxes.

THE WILD SIDE

IMAGE: A tiger at the London Zoo.

AMAZING ANIMALS

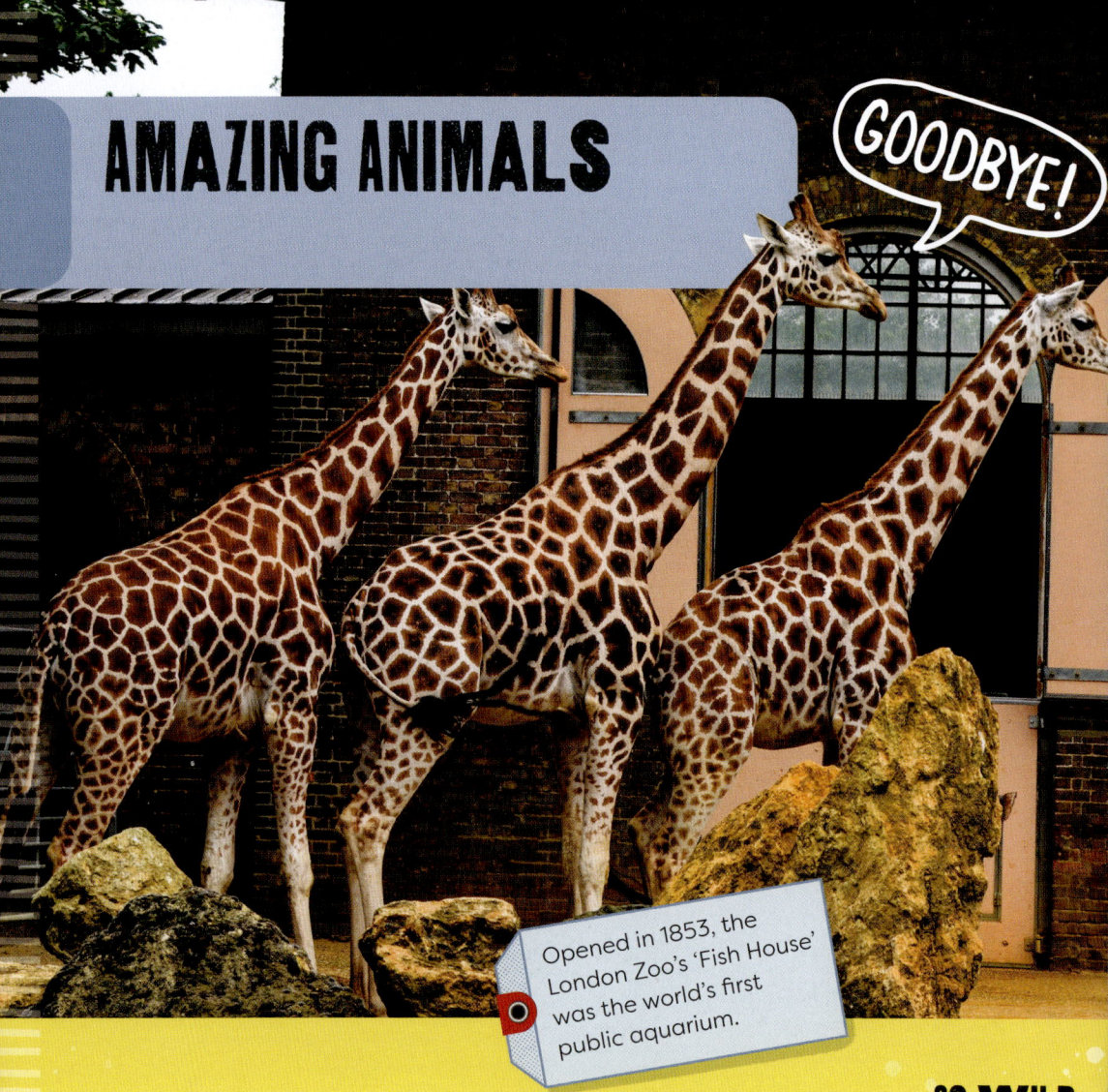

GOODBYE!

Opened in 1853, the London Zoo's 'Fish House' was the world's first public aquarium.

GO WILD

Animal lovers should make sure not to miss **London Zoo**, home to more than 10,000 animals! Come face-to-face with a silverback gorilla, watch African wild dogs play or listen to lions roar. You can also find out how the 200-year-old zoo cares for endangered animals – such as Sumatran tigers – and how scientists help reintroduce animals into the wild.

IMAGES: Giraffes at London Zoo (above); a variety of fish at the London Aquarium (opposite top); an old illustration of the zoo at the Tower of London (opposite bottom).

DIVE IN!

The **SEA LIFE London Aquarium** is home to over 6,000 animals. Here, you get more than just a glimpse at ocean life. Rays, sharks, penguins and seals are just a few of the creatures you'll encounter. And don't miss the underwater glass tunnel! Look up to see majestic sea creatures swim right above you! Then there's the shark walk, a glass floor where you can watch sharks swim just inches beneath your feet.

A TOWERING ZOO

Though the zoo at the Tower of London (see pages 74-75) no longer exists, wild animals lived there for about 600 years. In 1252, King Henry III was gifted a large white bear, most likely a polar bear, by the king of Norway. The bear was allowed to swim and hunt for fish in the Thames!

Make a Splash

A popular place to take a dip in north London is **Hampstead Heath**, a wild park famed for its ponds and pools – and less than 6.4 km (4 miles) from the city's centre.

The first recorded mention of the heath was in history books in 1543, when the springs fed water to London. At the time, it was forbidden for people to hunt here. The only hunting party allowed was that of King Henry III. Later, artists and authors began to visit the heath, a type of natural grassland. The land became a protected park in the 1800s.

Here, archaeologists have found tools used by people living in the area thousands of years ago in the Stone Age. Hampstead Heath is also said to have inspired author C.S. Lewis to write The Chronicles of Narnia.

Today, it includes three natural ponds perfect for swimming, but be warned: the water can get very cold! There's also Hampstead Heath's lido, an open-air, human-made pool perfect for a splash!

IMAGE: Swimming pond at Hampstead Heath.

Fast Facts

Size of Hampstead Heath: **320 hectares (790 acres)**

Number of butterfly species: **28**

Number of bird species: **180**

WILD INDOORS

DINO-MITE
Rainy day? Never fear – you can still get wild at the **Natural History Museum**. It's home to a 25-m (82-ft) blue whale skeleton! Here, you can go back in time to when reptiles ruled or view precious gems and minerals in the Earth's Treasury gallery. The museum's collection is huge – it owns 80 million objects! To study and care for so many pieces, the museum employs 900 staff.

Don't miss the Natural History Museum's Imilac meteorite, a gem as old as the known universe.

GET CREATIVE
The land where the **Dulwich Picture Gallery** now sits was once owned by Edward Alleyn, a famous actor in the 1600s and a favourite of Queen Elizabeth I. Today, it's home to 600 painted masterpieces. When the gallery opened in 1817, it was the first ever public art gallery. There's also something unexpected here: a mausoleum where the three original founders are buried.

BLAST TO THE PAST

You'll feel like you're travelling back in time at the **British Museum**, which showcases two million years of history around the globe. This iconic London destination is more than 250 years old! It's been around since 1753 and takes the title of oldest national public museum in the world. The museum was also home to a resident cat named Mike, who guarded the building from 1909 until 1929!

BIG IDEAS

It's time to hit the big screen – the *really* big screen, that is! London's **BFI IMAX** is the largest screen in London, measuring 20 m (66 ft) in both height and width – about as high as five double-decker buses! It gives viewers an immersive movie-going experience with nature films that take you across the icy Arctic, to the Moon or deep under the sea. There are blockbuster flicks, too!

IMAGES: A whale skeleton inside the Natural History Museum (opposite top); inside the Dulwich Picture Gallery (opposite bottom); a reconstruction of a seventh-century helmet at the British Museum (above); outside BFI IMAX (right).

WILD ABOUT LONDON

CITY LIFE

London may be a bustling city, but it's also full of wildlife, especially birds. No matter where you are – from the city's urban areas to its green expanses – you're sure to spot pigeons and sparrows. But if you keep your eyes peeled, you might also glimpse little owls, geese, kingfishers, falcons, starlings or parakeets. London's many parks are home to red foxes, deer, hedgehogs and European badgers, as well as plenty of pollinators like bees and bats. Admire from a distance!

There are an estimated 10,000 foxes around London.

Fast Facts

Number of deer species in London: **6**

Number of plant and animal species in London: **14,000**

Percentage of London covered in vegetation or water: **about 48**

Britain is home to only one kind of wildcat: the Scottish wildcat.

CREATURE FEATURE

Want to embark on your very own wildlife safari? Check out some of the top places around London to spot local animals. First stop: **Bushy Park**, a Royal Park (see pages 94–95). Here, keep your eyes open to spot deer and hedgehogs, as well as plenty of snakes, insects and birds. Next, venture over to the **London Wetland Centre** to see rare birds, such as sand martins, redshanks and bitterns. And don't forget to pop by the otter habitat – though they're not native, you won't want to miss the playful Asian short-clawed otters! Finally, make your way to the **Greenwich Peninsula Ecology Park** to scope out frogs, newts and even dragonflies.

IMAGES: A red fox in a London yard (above); a red deer at Bushy Park (left).

SUPER CELEBRATIONS

FANTASTIC FIREWORKS

If you happen to be in London for New Year's Eve – lucky you! The city puts on a world-famous fireworks show over the Thames near the London Eye (see pages 48–49) during which thousands of fireworks soar high. The raucous blasts are accompanied by the ringing of Big Ben (see pages 80–81) at midnight.

WELCOME THE LUNAR NEW YEAR

Typically celebrated in late January or early February, the Lunar New Year – often called Chinese New Year – marks the first new Moon of the lunisolar calendar and is celebrated in many places across China and eastern Asia. Join in on Lunar New Year celebrations in London's West End, where people celebrate with parades, costumes, large puppets, music and dancing.

IMAGES: Fireworks over Parliament (above); a dragon puppet at a Lunar New Year celebration (left); a dancer at Notting Hill Carnival (opposite top); Diwali celebrations at Trafalgar Square (opposite bottom).

COLOURFUL CARNIVAL

First held in 1966, the Notting Hill Carnival celebrates the history and influence of Caribbean culture in London. Usually held on the last weekend in August, festivities include enormous parades to upbeat music, traditional Caribbean food and drink and brightly coloured costumes.

More than one million people attend the Notting Hill Carnival each year.

DANCE AT DIWALI

Head to Trafalgar Square (see pages 78-79) during the fall to celebrate Diwali, a Hindu holiday known as the Festival of Lights. One of the largest holidays in India, Diwali is now celebrated in many places across the world, including London. See comedy, dance and puppet shows, join in on parades and stroll the stalls to sample delicious food.

GOING GREEN

IMAGE: Swans, geese and ducks in a London park.

A WALK IN THE PARK

HYDE-AND-SEEK

The largest of central London's eight Royal Parks (see pages 94–95), **Hyde Park** is a stunning space with an awesome history. The grounds were first used by the monks of Westminster Abbey. In 1536, King Henry VIII took over the land and made the spot one of his many hunting grounds. The grounds were later redesigned by Queen Caroline in the 1700s and then again in 1851 for London's international fair, the Great Exhibition. The 1851 exhibition hall took 5,000 workers five months to build!

IMAGES: Relaxing at Hyde Park (above); Hyde Park Winter Wonderland (opposite top); an illustration of Karl Marx (opposite bottom).

'TIS THE SEASON

Is it a hot and humid summer? Or maybe it's a chilly and wintry day? No matter the time of year, Hyde Park is always in season. Summer concerts entertain crowds; past performers have included legendary bands, such as Queen and the Rolling Stones. And **Serpentine Lake** is the perfect place to cool off with a swim. It gets it's name because its long and narrow – like a snake! In the winter, the lake is the site of a swim race that takes place on Christmas Day. Brrr!

Serpentine Lake extends into Kensington Gardens, where it goes by a different name: the Long Water.

THE PEOPLE'S PARK

Hyde Park has a lot of history. The **Speaker's Corner** has been the traditional site for public speeches, protests and demonstrations since the 1870s. Though the site sprang from gruesome origins – it was located near an area where prisoners were often executed – it became an important location in London's history, hosting suffragettes, public debates and speeches from political philosophers, such as Karl Marx.

GO GREENWICH

CHANGING GROUNDS

As the oldest enclosed Royal Park of London (see pages 94–95), this tranquil green space is also one of the city's most historic sites. A sixth-century Saxon burial ground, **Greenwich Park** was enclosed in 1433 and later became another one of King Henry VIII's hunting grounds in the 1500s. It was transformed again in the 1600s and then landscaped with grassy lawns, avenues of trees and flower beds before being opened to the public in the 1800s. Historians think that some of the deer now in the park may be the descendants of deer first brought to the area by Henry VIII.

IMAGES: The Queen's House museum at Greenwich Park (right); Greenwich Park Royal Observatory (below).

The Royal Observatory's Shepherd Gate Clock shows 24 hours on its face instead of 12.

Fast Facts

Size of the telescope lens: **71 cm (28 in)**

Size of the telescope tube: **8.5 m (28 ft)**

Number of double stars, or star pairs, glimpsed: **150,000**

STUDY THE SKIES

The **Royal Observatory** was built in Greenwich Park in 1675. It first served as a private observatory for the royal astronomer John Flamsteed, who made more than 50,000 observations of the Moon and stars. Today, the historic building showcases the latest in astronomy, as well as tools used long ago. The Great Equatorial Telescope, which aligns with the Earth's axis and moves parallel with the equator, rotates from east to west to view the moving night sky. The planetarium is where you want to be to marvel at the stars. The Greenwich meridian (a prime meridian) is also located here. It's the place geographers use as the starting point to measure distances east and west around the globe.

Going Green

RACE TO REGENT'S PARK

PARK PERFECTION

Designed in the early 1800s, **Regent's Park** is often considered the most elegant of all the Royal Parks (see pages 94–95). Like many other open spaces, it got its start as one of King Henry VIII's hunting grounds in the 1500s. Then, in the 1600s, the park was transformed from thick forest to wide-open space when most of the trees were chopped down during a civil war. Today, the original park is nearly unrecognisable with its now manicured collection of gardens and lawns.

Before it became a park, the woods of Regent's Park were often filled with wolves.

HEAD FOR THE HILL

Just north of Regent's Park, you can climb **Primrose Hill**: one of the highest natural spots in London. It has incredible views of the city skyline. The grassy lawns are popular for picnics and taking in the scene. Of course, while the hill is peaceful now, it wasn't always so. This was once a popular spot for duels!

RIOTS OF ROSES

With six gardens in Regent's Park, it can be tough to pick just one – but if you have limited time, be sure to stop by **Queen Mary's Gardens**. Here, some 12,000 roses bloom across 85 rose beds during the summer months. The blooms also attract wonderful wildlife, such as butterflies and other pollinators.

SUPER SPORTS

Regent's Park is home to the largest outdoor sports area in London. Many sports are played here including rugby, football, cricket, lacrosse, softball, tennis and much more. **Boating Lake** is often filled with bright-blue pedal boats and rowboats. A unique feature of this park in the heart of London is a special pond just for kids.

IMAGES: The Italian Gardens in Regent's Park (opposite top); relaxing on Primrose Hill (opposite bottom); roses in Queen Mary's Gardens (above); Boating Lake in Regent's Park (right).

INTO THE WILDERNESS

Many of London's Royal Parks (see pages 94-95) are known for their manicured lawns, stately flower beds and picturesque fountains. But **Richmond Park**, located in southwest London, is famous for its untamed wilderness.

The park's royal history dates back to the 1200s, when it was part of a royal manor. In 1625, a terrible plague swept through London – one of many waves of the plague that would strike the city that century. To avoid the illness, King Charles I moved his entire court to Richmond Palace. He also officially declared the grounds as Richmond Park.

In 1637, King Charles I had a wall built to keep the public out. However, people became so angry that the king installed a ladder on the wall to allow them in again!

Today, Richmond Park is home to ancient oak trees, as well as its large herd of wild red and fallow deer that often lounge around.

> Some of the anthills in Richmond Park are more than 200 years old!

IMAGE: A group of deer in Richmond Park.

Fast Facts

Park size: **1,000 hectares (2,500 acres)**

Number of deer in the park: **more than 600**

Number of anthills: **around 400,000**

SECRETS OF THE CITY

IMAGE: Shops in Camden Market.

GO UNDERGROUND

When it was in service, the Mail Rail delivered mail for 22 hours a day.

POST WITH THE MOST

Before there were emails, people mostly corresponded by snail mail, or physical letters and messages. But how did all that paper get from point A to point B? The **Postal Museum** answers that question and more: people delivered the mail using mail buses and horse-drawn carriages. One of the best parts of this stop is the Underground Railway, or Mail Rail. Visitors can hop on the historic Mail Rail for a ride that takes you through London's abandoned transport tunnels.

IMAGES: A British Royal Mail horse-drawn coach at the Postal Museum (above); London Mithraeum (opposite top); inside the Guildhall Art Gallery (opposite bottom).

HIDDEN BELOW

Have you ever wondered what secrets could be hiding underneath your feet? For the residents of one London neighbourhood, the answer was two-fold: a lost river and a Roman ruin. The **London Mithraeum** includes the ruins of a Roman temple that's more than 1,700 years old and was once located along the banks of London's River Walbrook. It's a wonder to explore! This temple belonged to the cult of Mithras, a mysterious and secretive Roman religious group. Though the ancient Romans are long gone, you can still see artefacts left behind.

The River Walbrook still runs – only it is entirely underground. It flows south into the Thames.

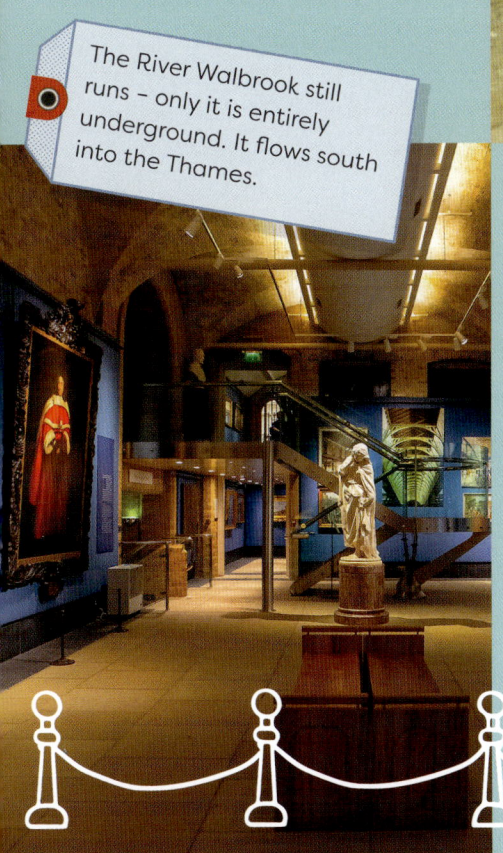

ROMAN REMAINS

The **Guildhall Art Gallery** is home to a rich collection of Victorian paintings and other spectacular pieces of art. It also hides a secret – a gruesome history deep underground. Here, there are ruins of a Roman amphitheatre nearly 2,000 years old, where ancient Romans flocked to see violent gladiator battles, animal fights and public executions.

The Roman amphitheatre could fit around 6,000 spectators.

Must-see Markets

London's many indoor and outdoor markets are bursting with tasty snacks, colourful wares, surprising finds and perhaps even hidden treasures. **Borough Market** has existed for more than 1,000 years and continues to be a great place to find fresh produce and other tasty treats. In the 13th century, London briefly banned its citizens from shopping at Borough Market – then located outside of London – so that people would spend their money within the city.

At **Camden Market** vendors and artists sell everything from clothes to toys to pet accessories. This market has also played a big part in Britain's music scene. A dance hall located at the market is where many of history's famous punk bands, from The Clash to Blondie, had their debut gigs.

Then there is **Portobello Road Market**, one of the world's largest antique markets – there are 1,500 stalls selling everything from antique watches to ancient furniture. This market has been around since the 19th century.

IMAGE: Camden Market at nighttime.

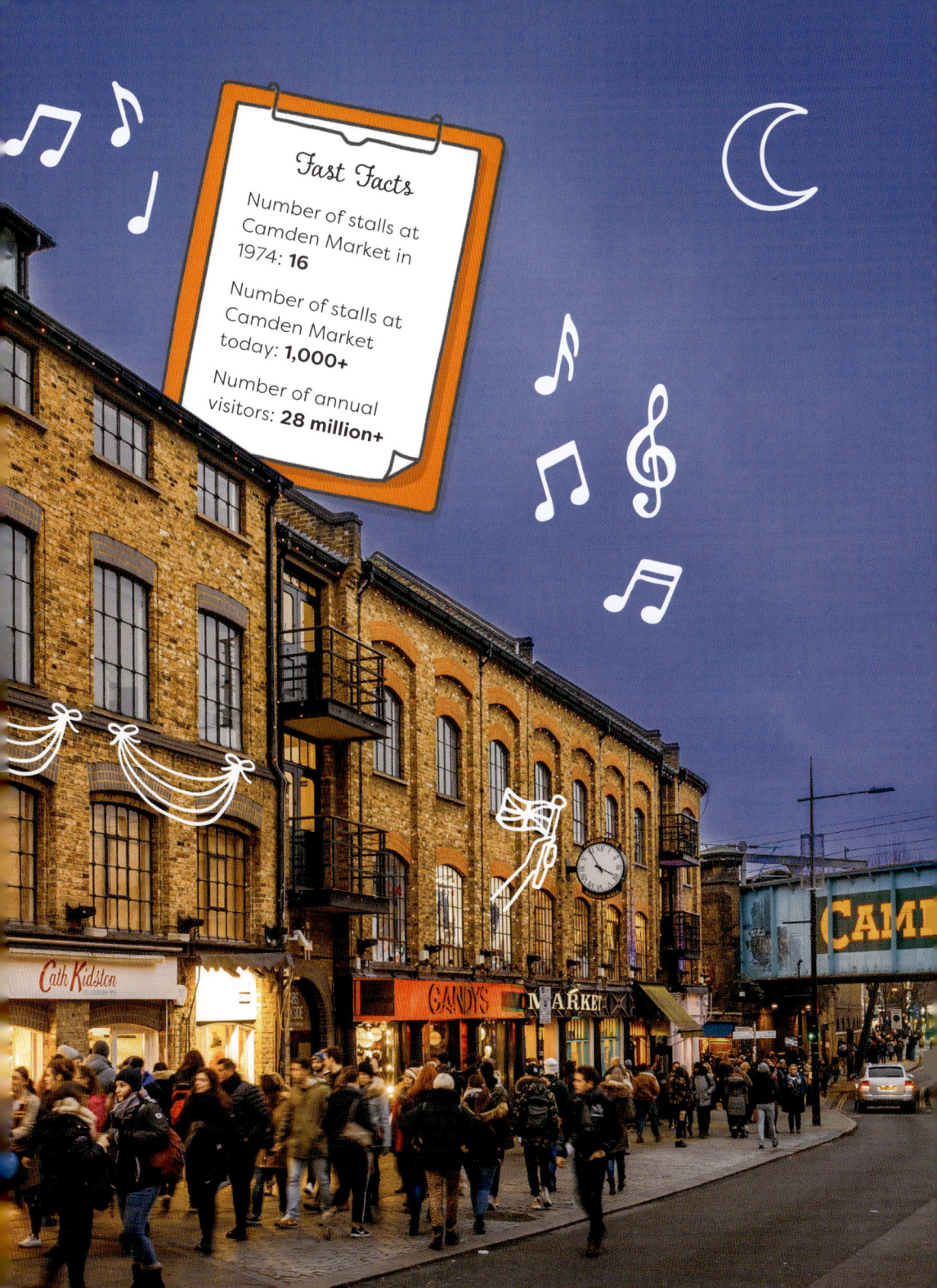

Fast Facts

Number of stalls at Camden Market in 1974: **16**

Number of stalls at Camden Market today: **1,000+**

Number of annual visitors: **28 million+**

SCARE YOURSELF SILLY

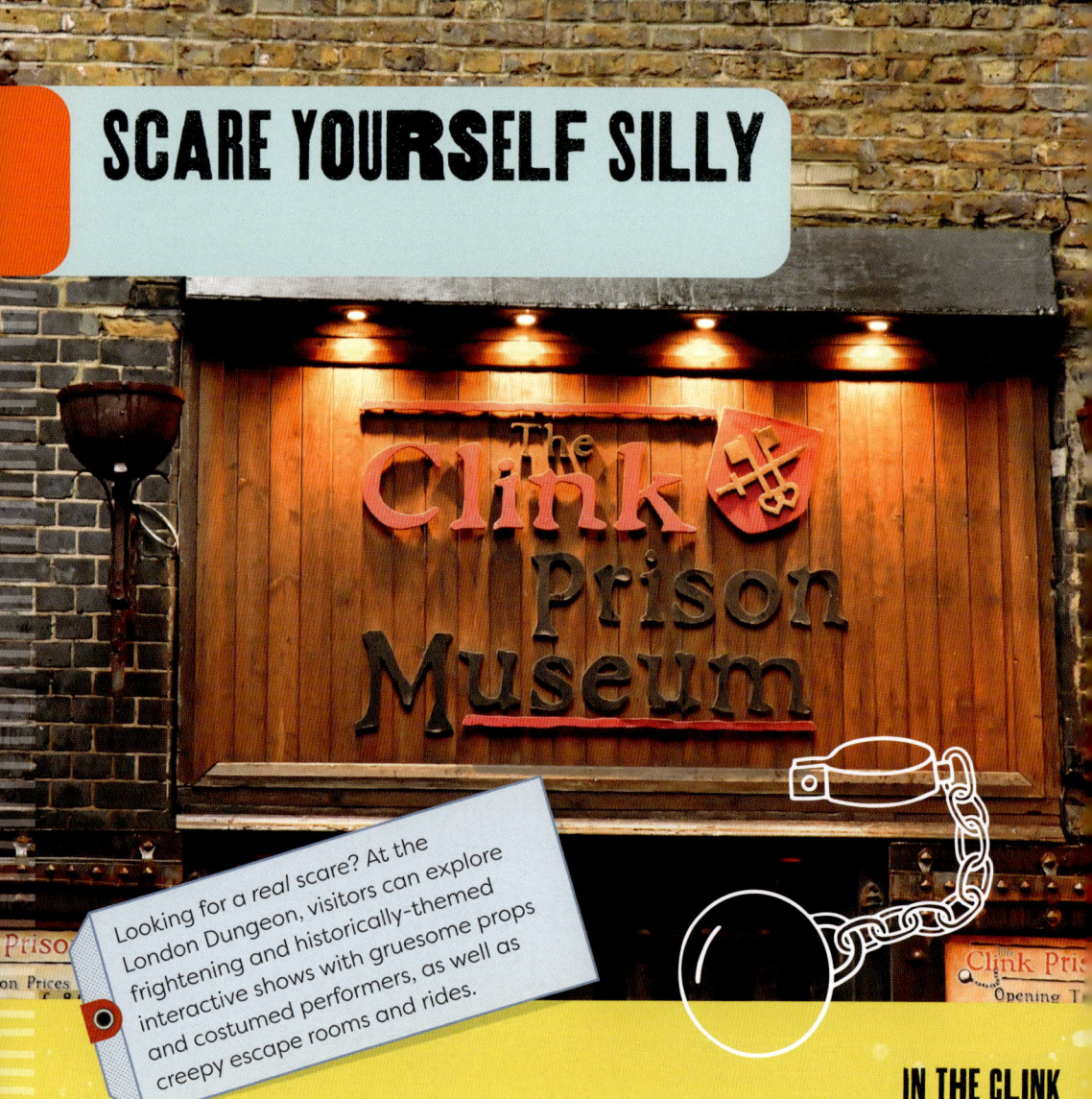

Looking for a real scare? At the London Dungeon, visitors can explore frightening and historically-themed interactive shows with gruesome props and costumed performers, as well as creepy escape rooms and rides.

IN THE CLINK

Built on the site of one of London's oldest prisons, the **Clink Prison Museum** guides visitors through the grisly history of London's crime and punishments. First opened in 1144, the Clink Prison operated until 1780 and became notorious for its harsh penalties and awful conditions. Today, the original cells are open to visitors to learn about the prison's hairy history.

IMAGES: The Clink Prison Museum (above); mausoleums at Highgate Cemetery (opposite top); historic medicine containers at the Old Operating Theatre (opposite bottom).

GO GOTHIC

Established in 1839, **Highgate Cemetery** has become a popular tourist destination for its eerie, Gothic atmosphere and elaborately designed tombs. Here, Egyptian Avenue is a collection of funerary vaults designed to look like ancient Egyptian temples. The Circle of Lebanon is a circular group of tombs that once surrounded a centuries-old tree. The cemetery also holds the resting places of many celebrities, authors, musicians and politicians.

Housed in the church at St Thomas's Hospital is a space once used to dry and store herbs such as wormwood and dragon's blood, which were used for medicine.

THE DOCTOR IS IN

Located in the attic of an 18th-century hospital, the **Old Operating Theatre** can only be accessed by climbing up a narrow spiral staircase of 52 steps. Here, in the attic of the church inside St Thomas's Hospital, you'll lay your eyes on the oldest existing operating theatre in Europe. Learn about the often ghastly history of surgery in London and find out how doctors operated at a time when there was no way to prevent patients from feeling pain during procedures. There are also old operating devices, from bone saws to operating tables.

Secrets of the City 125

SOLVE MYSTERIES

HOLMES SWEET HOLMES

Step into 221B Baker Street – the address of Sherlock Holmes, England's most famous detective and the star of the fictional book series written by Sir Arthur Conan Doyle. Since the first Sherlock Holmes story was published in 1887, the supersleuth has appeared in countless television shows and films. Dive into the world of Sherlock Holmes by visiting the **Sherlock Holmes Museum**, a 19th-century town house transformed to look like Holmes's lodgings. Inside are items related to some of Holmes's most famous cases and even some life-size wax figures.

IMAGES: Inside the Sherlock Holmes Museum (right); Temple Church (below).

Fast Facts

Number of Sherlock Holmes stories: **56**

First Sherlock Holmes story: **A Study in Scarlet**

Number of Sherlock Holmes titles sold: **60 million+**

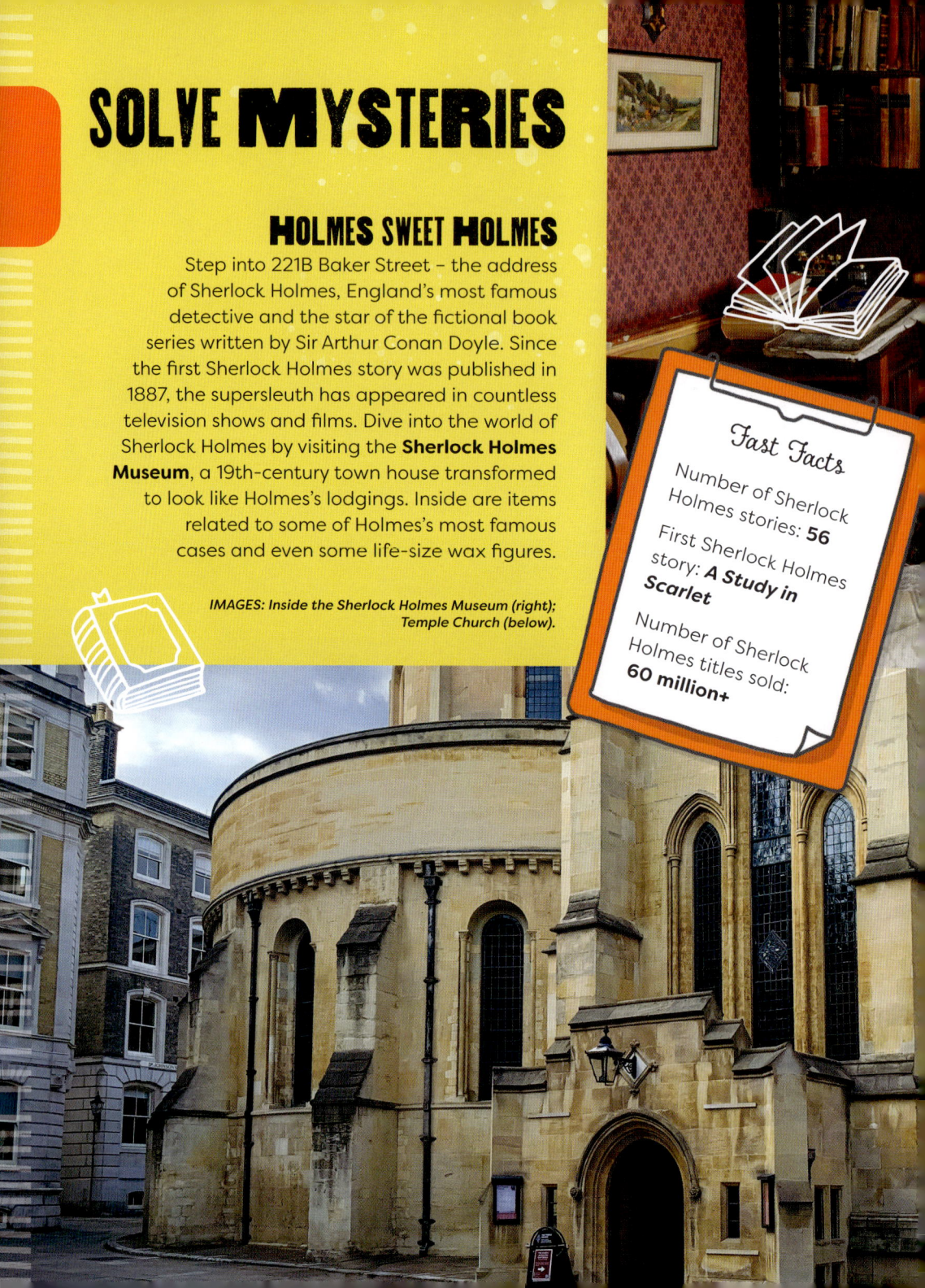

Some companies offer Sherlock Holmes–themed tours of London, stopping at locations mentioned in the book series or places used for filming the shows and films.

SEARCH FOR LOST TREASURE

One of the oldest churches in London, **Temple Church** is also one of the most storied. This church was built in the 12th century by the Knights Templar, a religious order of knights famous for their secret ceremonies and rites. Over time, the Templars grew in power – and so did rumours of the knights' wealth. In 1307, perhaps wanting the supposed riches for himself, King Philip IV of France called for the Templars to be arrested. The Templars were disbanded throughout Europe – but, according to legend, not before they hid their massive collection of gold and jewels. The Temple Church remains; visitors can view the historic architecture and perhaps even search for clues to the supposed missing treasure!

LIFE OF LUXURY

HOP OVER TO HARRODS

No London shopping day is complete without a visit to **Harrods**. Harrods got its start in 1824, when merchant Charles Henry Harrod opened a small grocery store. Since then, Harrods has become a London staple, as well as a luxury department store. It's also known for having England's first escalator, which was considered an engineering marvel at the time it was installed in 1898.

WHAT'S IN STORE

First founded in 1875, **Liberty of London**, or Liberty's as it is commonly known, is a must-see for fashionistas and history fans alike. On top of being renowned for its unique, hand-drawn fabrics, the department store is famed for the building in which it resides. Constructed in 1924, the building was designed in the Tudor Revival style (that is, made to look like the buildings popular in the 16th century) and made from the timbers of three historic battleships.

IMAGES: Outside Harrods (above); inside Liberty of London (left); teddy bears dressed like Buckingham Palace Guards at Hamleys (opposite top); Word on the Water (opposite bottom).

TOTALLY TOYS

Hamleys is more than just a toy store. Sure, it sells almost every toy you can think of. And, yes, the flagship location has seven stories full of toys. But on top that, Hamleys is full of history. In fact, it is the oldest existing toy store in the world! Hamleys first opened as Noah's Ark toy store all the way back in 1760 by a man named William Hamley. The store soon became so popular it opened in several more locations – and survived over the centuries to become an international icon.

In the early 1900s, Hamleys often delivered items to customers' doorsteps using horse-drawn carriages.

BOAT OF BOOKS

Is **Word on the Water** a bookstore or a boat? It's both! Step onto this historic barge to browse a selection of books – or if you prefer to stay on dry land, you can peruse parts of the bookstore from the street. In the past, Word on the Water floated from spot to spot, but today it can be found at a set location on Regent's Canal. In warmer weather, the store also hosts live music, poetry readings and more.

WHAT'S THE DIFFERENCE?

The red telephone box is an iconic London sight. Can you spot the five differences between these two pictures? See answers on page 140.

WHAT'S THE DIFFERENCE?

Tower Bridge is one of the most famous views in the city. Can you spot the five differences between these two pictures? See answers on page 140.

INDEX

A
Abbey Road 24
Albert, Prince 90
Alleyn, Edward 102
amusement parks and rides 40-41, **40-41**, 48-49, **48-49**
animals 96-105. *See also* zoos
    Hampstead Heath 101
    Horniman Butterfly House 35
    Kew Palace 91
    in parks and gardens 37, 104-105, **104-105, 108-109,** 114
    red fox **104-105**
    River Thames 66, 73, **73,** 99
    St James's Park 95
aquarium 99, **99**
ArcelorMittal Orbit 48-49, **48-49**
art museums. *See* museums
Athelstan, King 72

B
Bank of England 43
Bawcock, Tom 67
Beatles (band) 24
beef Wellington 63, **63**
Belfast, HMS 83, **83**
BFI IMAX 103, **103**
bicycling 24-25, **24-25**
Big Ben **12-13, 14,** 78, 80-81, **80-81,** 106
biscuits 68-69, **68-69**
black cabs (taxis) 21, **21**
black pudding 67, **67**
Boating Lake 115, **115**
Boleyn, Anne 75, **75**
Borough Market 122
British Museum 103, **103**
Brompton Cemetery 94
Buckingham Palace **86**
    basics 86
    Changing of the Guard ceremony **8-9,** 87, **87**
    King's Gallery 92-93, **92-93**
    on map **14**
    Queen's Birthday Parade **84-85**
    Royal Collection 86, 92-93, **92-93**
    Royal Mews (stables) 78, 87, **87**
Burnt Stub Mansion 41
buses
    bus system 20
    double-decker buses **12-13, 18-19,** 20, **20,** 21, **21, 34,** 60
    hop-on hop-off tours 21, **21**
    river buses 30
Bushy Park **104-105,** 105

C
cable car 28-29, **28-29**
cabs 21, **21**
Camden Market **118-119,** 122-123, **122-123**
Caroline, Queen 95, 110
catacombs 94
Changing of the Guard ceremony **8-9,** 87, **87**
Charles I, King 92, 116
Charles II, King 94
Charlotte, Queen 91
Chessington World of Adventures Resort 41, **41**
chicken tikka masala 64, **64-65**
Chinese New Year 106, **106**
Chronicles of Narnia, The (Lewis) 100
Chunnel 28-29, **28-29**
civil wars 92, 114
climbing 52, 53
Clink Prison Museum 124, **124**
concert venues **15,** 52-53, **52-53,** 111, 122
Covent Garden 55, **55**
Crown Jewels 75, **75**
Crystal Palace Park 36, **36**
Cutty Sark 83, **83**
cycling 24-25, **24-25**

D
Diana, Princess of Wales Memorial Playground 37, **37**
Diwali celebrations 107, **107**
Docklands Light Railway (DLR) 23, **23**
double-decker buses **12-13, 18-19,** 20, **20,** 21, **34,** 60
Doyle, Sir Arthur Conan 126
Drake, Sir Francis 82
Dulwich Picture Gallery 102, **102**

E
Edward I, King 74
Edward VI, King 81
Elizabeth I, Queen 68, 91, 102
Elizabeth II, Queen **88-89,** 93
Elizabeth line 22, **22**
Elizabeth Tower. *See* Big Ben
Ethelred, King 72
Eton mess **58-59**
Eurotunnel train **28-29**

F
Ferris wheels **15,** 46-47, **46-47,** 48-49, **48-49**
festivals 106-107, **106-107**

film sites **32-33**, 42-43, **42-43**
finger sandwiches 60, **60-61**
fire (1666) 76, 77
fireworks 106, **106**
fish and chips 62, **62**
Flamsteed, John 113
Fleming, Sir Alexander 76
food 58-69
    beef Wellington 63, **63**
    biscuits (cookies) 68-69, **68-69**
    black pudding 67, **67**
    chicken tikka masala 64, **64-65**
    fish and chips 62, **62**
    full English breakfast 62, **62**
    fusion 64-65, **64-65**
    jellied eels 66, **66**
    puddings (desserts) 68, **68-69**
    stargazy pie 67, **67**
    sweet treats **58-59**, 68-69, **68-69**
    tea 60, **60-61**
    unusual 66-67, **66-67**
    Yorkshire pudding 63, **63**

G
gardens. *See* parks and gardens
George I, King 90
George III, King 91, 92, 93
George IV, King 86
Gherkin **15**
gingerbread men 68, **68**
Globe Theatre 44, **44**
Golden Hinde 82, **82**
Great Britain 15
Great Exhibition 110
great fire of London 76, 77
Green Park 94, **94**
Greenwich Park 112-113, **112-113**
Greenwich Peninsula Ecology Park 105
Guildhall Art Gallery 121, **121**

H
hackney carriages (taxis) 21, **21**
Hamleys toy store 129, **129**
Hampstead Heath 100-101, **100-101**
Hampton Court Palace 91, **91**
Harrod, Charles Henry 128
Harrods 128, **128**
Harry, Prince 90
Harry Potter **32-33**, 42-43, **42-43**
Henry III, King 74, 99, 100
Henry VIII, King 75, 91, 95, 110, 112, 114
Highgate Cemetery 125, **125**
holidays 106-107, **106-107**
Horniman Museum & Gardens 35, **35**
Houses of Parliament **14**, 27, 80-81, **80-81**, 106
Hyde Park 110-111, **110-111**

I
IFS Cloud Cable Car 28-29, **28-29**

J
jellied eels 66, **66**
Jonas Brothers **52-53**

K
Kate, Princess of Wales 90
Kensington Gardens 43, 111
Kensington Palace 90, **90**, 95
Kew Gardens 91
Kew Palace 91, **91**
King's Cross Station 43, **43**
King's Gallery 92-93, **92-93**
Knights Templar 127

L
Lee Valley Regional Park 37, **37**
LEGOLAND Windsor Resort 41, **41**
Lewis, C.S. 100
Liberty of London 128, **128**
Londinium 13, 72
London Aquarium 99, **99**
London Bridge 51
London Dungeon 124
London Eye **15**, **46-47**, 48-49, **48-49**
London Mithraeum 121, **121**
London Overground 23, **23**
London Transport Museum 34, **34**
London Underground (Tube) 10, 16, **16-17**, 26-27, **26-27**
London Wetland Centre 105
London Zoo **96-97**, 98, **98**
Lunar New Year 106, **106**

M
map **14-15**
markets **118-119**, 122-123, **122-123**
Marx, Karl 111, **111**
Mary II, Queen 90
Mary Poppins 43
Meghan, Duchess of Sussex 90
Michelangelo 93
Millennium Bridge **70-71**
movie sites **32-33**, 42-43, **42-43**
museums
    Aldwych ghost station 26
    British Museum 103, **103**
    Clink Prison Museum 124, **124**
    Dulwich Picture Gallery 102, **102**
    Guildhall Art Gallery 121, **121**
    Horniman Museum & Gardens 35, **35**
    King's Gallery 92-93, **92-93**
    London Transport Museum 34, **34**
    National Maritime Museum 82, **82**
    National Portrait Gallery 79, **79**
    Natural History Museum 102, **102**

INDEX

Postal Museum 120, **120**
Queen's House museum **113**
Royal Academy of Arts 93, **93**
Science Museum 34, **34**
Sherlock Holmes Museum 126-127, **126-127**
Tate Modern 56-57, **56-57**
Victoria and Albert Museum 56-57, **56-57**
Wimbledon Lawn Tennis Museum 38
Young V&A 35, **35**

N
National Maritime Museum 82, **82**
National Portrait Gallery 79, **79**
Natural History Museum 102, **102**
Nelson's Column 78
Notting Hill Carnival 107, **107**

O
O2 Arena **15**, 52-53, **52-53**
Old Operating Theatre 125, **125**

P
Paddington Bear **42-43**, 43
Paddington Station **42-43**, 43
Palace of Westminster. See Houses of Parliament
parks and gardens
    amusement parks and rides 40-41, **40-41**, 48-49, **48-49**
    Brompton Cemetery 94
    Bushy Park **104-105**, 105
    Crystal Palace Park 36, **36**
    Diana, Princess of Wales Memorial Playground 37, **37**
    Green Park 94, **94**
    Greenwich Park 112-113, **112-113**
    Greenwich Peninsula Ecology Park 105
    Hampstead Heath 100-101, **100-101**
    Horniman Museum & Gardens 35
    Hyde Park 110-111, **110-111**
    Kensington Gardens 95, **95**, 111
    Lee Valley Regional Park 37, **37**
    London Wetland Centre 105
    Primrose Hill 114, **114**
    Queen Mary's Gardens 115, **115**
    Regent's Park 114-115, **114-115**
    Richmond Park 116-117, **116-117**
    Royal Parks 94, **94**, 104-105, 105, 110-117, **110-117**
    St James's Park 95, **95**
    wildlife 37, 104-105, **104-105**, **108-109**, 114
Parliament. See Houses of Parliament

pedicabs 24
Peter Pan 43
Philip IV, King of France 127
Piccadilly Circus 55, **55**
Portobello Road Market 122
Postal Museum 120, **120**
Primrose Hill 114, **114**
puddings (desserts) 68, **68-69**
Puppet Theatre Barge 45, **45**

Q
Queen Mary's Gardens 115, **115**
Queen's House museum **113**

R
Regent Street **24-25**, **26-27**
Regent's Canal 43, 45, **45**, 129, **129**
Regent's Park 114-115, **114-115**
Richmond Park 116-117, **116-117**
River Thames. See Thames
Roman history 13, 22, 72, 121, **121**
Royal Academy of Arts 93, **93**
Royal Docks **28-29**
Royal Mews (stables) 78, 87, **87**
Royal Observatory 112-113, **112-113**
Royal Opera House (ROH) 45, **45**
Royal Parks 94, **94**, **104-105**, 105, 110-117, **110-117**

S
scary places 124-125, **124-125**
Science Museum 34, **34**
scones 60
Serpentine Lake 111
Shakespeare, William 79, 89
Shakespeare's Globe Theatre 44, **44**
Shard **15**, 54, **54**
Sherlock Holmes Museum 126-127, **126-127**
shopping
    luxury stores 128-129, **128-129**
    markets **118-119**, 122-123, **122-123**
Speaker's Corner 111
sports
    cycling 24-25, **24-25**
    Regent's Park 115, **115**
    swimming 100, **100-101**, 111
    tennis 38-39, **38-39**
St James's Park 95, **95**
St Paul's Cathedral **14**, 43, 76-77, **76-77**
St Thomas's Hospital 125, **125**
stargazy pie 67, **67**
swimming 100, **100-101**, 111

T
Tate Modern 56–57, **56–57**
taxis 21, **21**
tea 60, **60–61**
Templars 127
Temple Church **126–127,** 127
tennis 38–39, **38–39**
Thames **30–31**
    fireworks **106**
    history 72, **72,** 73, **73**
    IFS Cloud Cable Car 28–29, **28–29**
    on map **14–15**
    Millennium Bridge **70–71**
    pronunciation 12
    river buses 30
    shipwrecks 31
    sightseeing cruise 30
    Tower Bridge **15,** 50–51, **50–51,** 83
    wildlife 66, 73, **73,** 99
Thames Tunnel 23
theatres 44–45, **44–45**
Thorpe Park 40, **40**
Tower Bridge **15,** 50–51, **50–51,** 83
Tower of London **15,** 74–75, **74–75,** 99, **99**
Trafalgar Square 78–79, **78–79,** 87, 107, **107**
trains 22–23, **22–23,** 28–29, **28–29**. *See also* London Underground
trams 22, **22**
Tube. *See* London Underground
Twinings tea shop 60

U
Underground. *See* London Underground
United Kingdom 15

V
Victoria, Queen 86, 90
Vikings 76

W
walking 24–25, **24–25**
Warner Bros. Studio Tour London: The Making of *Harry Potter* **32–33,** 42–43, **42–43**
Waterloo Tube station 10
Westminster Abbey 12, **14,** 88–89, **88–89,** 110
Westminster Underground station 27
What's the Difference? **130–133, 140**
wildlife. *See* animals
William, Prince of Wales 90
William I (the Conqueror), King 72, 74, 88, 90
William III, King 90
Wiltshire maze 36
Wimbledon 38–39, **38–39**
Windsor Castle 90, **90**
Word on the Water bookstore 129, **129**
World War II 83

Y
Yorkshire pudding 63, **63**
Young V&A 35, **35**

Z
zoos
    Chessington World of Adventures Resort 41, **41**
    Crystal Palace Park petting zoo 36
    London Zoo **96–97,** 98, **98**
    Royal Menagerie 74
    Tower of London 99, **99**

RESOURCES & PHOTO CREDITS

Getting Around Town (pages 18-31)
Big Bus Tours: bigbustours.com
Footways: footways.london
Tootbus: tootbus.com/en
Transport for London: tfl.gov.uk

Places to Play (pages 32-45)
Chessington World of Adventures Resort: chessington.com
Horniman Museum & Gardens: horniman.ac.uk
Lee Valley Regional Park: visitleevalley.org.uk
LEGOLAND: legoland.co.uk
London Science Museum: sciencemuseum.org.uk
London Transport Museum: ltmuseum.co.uk
Puppet Theatre Barge: puppetbarge.com
Royal Opera House: roh.org.uk
Shakespeare's Globe Theatre: shakespearesglobe.com
Thorpe Park: thorpepark.com
Warner Bros. Studio Tour London: wbstudiotour.co.uk
Wimbledon: wimbledon.com
Wimbledon Village: wimbledonvillage.com
Young V&A: vam.ac.uk/young

What a View! (pages 46-57)
ArcelorMittal Orbit: arcelormittalorbit.com
Covent Garden: coventgarden.london
London Eye: londoneye.com
O2 Arena: theo2.co.uk
Tate Modern: tate.org.uk/visit/tate-modern
The Shard: the-shard.com
Tower Bridge: towerbridge.org.uk
Victoria and Albert Museum: vam.ac.uk

Let's Eat! (pages 58-69)
Twinings: twinings.co.uk

Along the Thames (pages 70-83)
Cutty Sark: rmg.co.uk/cutty-sark
Golden Hinde: goldenhinde.co.uk
HMS Belfast: iwm.org.uk/visits/hms-belfast
National Portrait Gallery: npg.org.uk
Palace of Westminster: parliament.uk
St Paul's Cathedral: stpauls.co.uk

The Royal Treatment (pages 84-95)
Historic Royal Palaces: hrp.org.uk
Royal Academy of Arts: royalacademy.org.uk
Royal Collection Trust: rct.uk
Royal Parks: royalparks.org.uk
The Royal Family: royal.uk
Westminster Abbey: westminster-abbey.org

The Wild Side (pages 96-107)
BFI IMAX: bfi.org.uk/bfi-imax
British Museum: britishmuseum.org
Diwali: diwaliinlondon.com
Dulwich Picture Gallery: dulwichpicturegallery.org.uk
Hampstead Heath: hampsteadheath.net
London Wetland Centre: wwt.org.uk/wetland-centres/london
London Wildlife Trust: wildlondon.org.uk
London Zoo: londonzoo.org
Natural History Museum: nhm.ac.uk
Notting Hill Carnival: nhcarnival.org
SEA LIFE London Aquarium: visitsealife.com/london

Going Green (pages 108-117)
Royal Observatory: rmg.co.uk/royal-observatory

Secrets of the City (pages 118-129)
Borough Market: boroughmarket.org.uk
Camden Market: camdenmarket.com
Clink Prison Museum: clink.co.uk
Guildhall Art Gallery: guildhall.cityoflondon.gov.uk
Hamleys: hamleys.com
Harrods: harrods.com
Highgate Cemetery: highgatecemetery.org
Liberty of London: libertylondon.com
London Mithraeum: londonmithraeum.com
Old Operating Theatre: oldoperatingtheatre.com
Portobello Road Market: portobelloroad.co.uk
Postal Museum: postalmuseum.org
Sherlock Holmes Museum: sherlock-holmes.co.uk
Temple Church: templechurch.com
Word on the Water: wordonthewater.co.uk

IMAGE CREDITS
Illustration © 2025 Carolyn Sewell
8-9: David Steele/Shutterstock / **12-13:** Sylvain Sonnet/Getty Images / **14-15:** Rainer Lesniewski/Shutterstock / **16-17:** VanderWolf Images/Shutterstock (Tube station); Studio MDF/Shutterstock (person looking at map) / **18-19:** Scott Barbour/Getty Images / **20:** Ron Ellis/Shutterstock / **21:** Kamira/Shutterstock (taxi); Lucian Milasan/Shutterstock (bus) / **22:** William Barton/Shutterstock (tram); Alex Segre/Shutterstock (inside car) / **23:** Jakub Rutkiewicz/Shutterstock (DLR); Nigel J. Harris/Shutterstock (Overground) / **24-25:** cowardlion/Shutterstock (bicycles); Alexander Spatari/Getty Images (Regent Street) / **26-27:** Andres Garcia Martin/Shutterstock / **28-29:** Andy Soloman/UCG/Universal Images Group via Getty Images (Chunnel); Abdul_Shakoor/Shutterstock (cable cars) / **30-31:** vladimir zakharov/Getty Images / **32-33:** 365_visuals/Shutterstock / **34:** goga18128/Shutterstock (buses); Marco Prati/Shutterstock (Science Museum) / **35:** David Parry/Shutterstock (costumes); Pav-Pro Photography Ltd/Shutterstock (Horniman) / **36:** Abdul_Shakoor/Shutterstock / **37:** Marcin Rogozinski/Alamy Stock Photo (horseback riding); cowardlion/Shutterstock (pirate ship) / **38-39:** Meaning March/Shutterstock / **40:** Angyalosi Beata/Shutterstock / **41:** Lukasz Sadlowski/Shutterstock (water ride); anastas_styles/Shutterstock (LEGOLAND) / **42-43:** chrisdorney/Shutterstock (bear); COO7/Shutterstock (Harry Potter); John Wreford/Shutterstock (King's Cross) / **44:** cowardlion/Shutterstock / **45:** N.M.Bear/Shutterstock (Royal Opera House); Alphotographic/Getty Images (Puppet Theatre Barge) / **46-47:** Valdis Skudre/Shutterstock / **48-49:** Abs fotos/Shutterstock (tower); Christian Mueller/Shutterstock (London Eye) / **50-51:** chbaum/Shutterstock / **52-53:** Richard Isaac/Shutterstock (Jonas Brothers); Aerial-motion/Shutterstock (roof) / **54:** zefart/Shutterstock / **55:** Roberto Lotti/500px/Getty Images (Covent Garden); Lukasz Pajor/Shutterstock (Piccadilly Circus) / **56-57:** Ralu Spatareanu/Shutterstock (costumes); Pawel Libera/Getty Images (Tate Modern) / **58-59:** Alexey Borodin/Shutterstock / **60-61:** Debra Angel/Shutterstock / **62:** neil langan/Shutterstock (fish and chips); Slawomir Fajer/Shutterstock (breakfast) / **63:** Goskova Tatiana/Shutterstock (beef Wellington); DronG/Shutterstock (pudding) / **64-65:** nelea33/Shutterstock (chicken tikka masala); DronG/Shutterstock (chow mein) / **66:** Monkey Business Images/Shutterstock / **67:** Davis Dorss/Shutterstock (pie); Joerg Beuge/Shutterstock (black pudding) / **68-69:** Alesia.Bierliezova/Shutterstock (gingerbread); Juven Tan/Shutterstock (shortbread) / alexanderon/Shutterstock (pie) / **70-71:** Claudio Divizia/Shutterstock / **72:** Museum of London/Heritage Images/Getty Images / **73:** Historia/Shutterstock (cartoon); Darren Baker/Shutterstock (swans) / **74:** Sergii Figurnyi/Shutterstock (bedchamber); Justin Black/Shutterstock (tower exterior) / **75:** Photos.com/Getty Images (portrait); John Harper/Getty Images (crown) / **76-77:** Dan Breckwoldt/Shutterstock / **78:** Marco Rubino/Shutterstock (lion); AlexKozlov/Getty Images (fountains) / **79:** Prettyawesome/Shutterstock (statue); Alex Segre/Shutterstock (gallery) / **80-81:** TangMan Photography/Getty Images (palace); Peter Nadolski/Shutterstock (clock face) / **82:** Botond Horvath/Shutterstock (*Golden Hinde*); Tom Meaker/Shutterstock (National Maritime Museum) / **83:** Pandora Pictures/Shutterstock (HMS *Belfast*); johnbraid/Shutterstock (*Cutty Sark*) / **84-85:** Watcharisma/Shutterstock / **86:** Tetra Images/Getty Images / **87:** Alexander Chaikin/Shutterstock (guard); Dave Goodman/Shutterstock (coach) / **88-89:** Danny Lawson - WPA Pool/Getty Images (Westminster Abbey); IR Stone/Shutterstock (tomb) / **90:** Mistervlad/Shutterstock (Kensington Palace); Kiev.Victor/Shutterstock (Windsor Castle) / **91:** Grant Faint/Getty Images (Hampton Court); Afflamen/Shutterstock (Kew Gardens) / **92:** Claudio Divizia/Shutterstock / **93:** William Barton/Shutterstock / **94:** Destinyweddingstudio/Shutterstock / **95:** mary416/Shutterstock (Kensington Gardens); ivanmateev/Getty Images (St James's Park) / **96-97:** Andywak/Shutterstock / **98:** Dair/Shutterstock / **99:** Nastasic/Getty Images (zoo); Endless luck/Shutterstock (fish) / **101-101:** Alex Segre/Getty Images / **102:** Alex Segre/Alamy Stock Photo (Dulwich Picture Gallery); pio3/Shutterstock (whale skeleton) / **103:** MAVRITSINA IRINA/Shutterstock (helmet); 4kclips/Shutterstock (theater) / **104-105:** AK-Media/Shutterstock (deer); Giedriius/Shutterstock (fox) / **106:** Alexey Fedorenko/Shutterstock (dragon); Samot/Shutterstock (fireworks) / **107:** Viktor Kovalenko/Shutterstock (Carnival); Lara Ra/Shutterstock (Diwali) / **108-109:** LanaG/Shutterstock / **110:** Arthur Tilley/Getty Images / **111:** Nicku/Shutterstock (Karl Marx); Marius_Comanescu/Shutterstock (ice-skating) / **112-113:** Pajor Pawel/Shutterstock (observatory); cowardlion/Shutterstock (Greenwich Park) / **114:** Simon McGill/Getty Images (Primrose Hill); Chrispictures/Shutterstock (Regent's Park) / **115:** chrisdorney/Shutterstock (roses); Daniele Silva/Shutterstock (lake) / **116-117:** Sampajano_Anizza/Shutterstock / **118-119:** Valdis Skudre/Shutterstock / **120:** Facundo Arrizabalaga/EPA/Shutterstock / **121:** cowardlion/Shutterstock (gallery); Peter_Fleming/Shutterstock (temple) / **122-123:** Maurizio De Mattei/Shutterstock / **124:** Pack-Shot/Shutterstock / **125:** Nataliia Zhekova/Shutterstock (containers); Dan Bridge/Getty Images (mausoleums) / **126-127:** Alla Tsyganova/Shutterstock (church); Anton_Ivanov/Shutterstock (museum) / **128:** Mykolastock/Shutterstock (Liberty's); Frank Gaertner/Shutterstock (Harrods) / **129:** Ink Drop/Shutterstock (teddy bears); Ingrid Pakats/Shutterstock (bookstore) / **130-131:** maziarz/Shutterstock / **132-133:** Sol de Zuasnabar Brebbia/Getty Images / **141:** giorgiogalano/Getty Images

WHAT'S THE DIFFERENCE? ANSWERS

140 A Kid's Guide to LONDON

IMAGE: Shops on Portobello Road.

The Portobello Road Market has been around for more than 150 years. Hundreds of vendors sell everything from century-old toys to ancient swords and golden jewels!